SRA
Reading
Mastery
Signature Edition

Literature Anthology

Siegfried Engelmann
Jean Osborn
Steve Osborn
Leslie Zoref

McGraw Hill SRA

Columbus, OH

Acknowledgments

Grateful acknowledgment is given to the following publishers and copyright owners for permissions granted to reprint selections from their publications. All possible care has been taken to trace ownership and secure permission for each selection included. In case of any errors or omissions, the Publisher will be pleased to make suitable acknowledgments in future editions.

Larry Bograd
"Willie and the Christmas Spruce" story by Larry Bograd. Used by permission of the author.

Farrar, Straus & Giroux
"Shrewd Todie & Lyzer the Miser" from STORIES FOR CHILDREN by Isaac Bashevis Singer. Copyright © 1984 by Isaac Bashevis Singer. Reprinted by permission of Farrar, Straus & Giroux, LLC.

Harcourt
"Trick or Treat" from LOCAL NEWS, copyright © 1993 by Gary Soto, reprinted by permission of Harcourt, Inc.

Holiday House
THE SHRINKING OF TREEHORN. Text copyright © 1971 by Florence Parry Heide. Illustrations copyright © 1971 by Edward Gorey. All rights reserved. Reprinted by permission of Holiday House, Inc.

Maria Carvainis Agency
From BLUE WILLOW by Pam Conrad, copyright © 1999 Pam Conrad. Used by permission of Maria Carvainis Agency.

Penguin Group (USA)
From BLUE WILLOW by Pam Conrad, illustrated by S. Saelig Gallagher, copyright © 1999 by Susan Saelig Gallager, illustrations. Used by permission of Philomel Books, A Division of Penguin Young Readers Group, A Member of Penguin Group (USA) Inc., 345 Hudson Street, New York, NY 10014. All rights reserved.
From THE GOLD CADILLAC by Mildred D. Taylor, copyright © 1987 BY Mildred D. Taylor, text. Used by permission of Dial Books for Young Readers, A Division of Penguin Young Readers Group, A Member of Penguin Group (USA) Inc., 345 Hudson Street, New York, NY 10014. All rights reserved.
From THE GOLD CADILLAC by Mildred D. Taylor, pictures by Michael Hays, copyright © 1987 by Michael Hays, pictures. Used by permission of Dial Books for Young Readers, A Division of Penguin Young Readers Group, A Member of Penguin Group (USA) Inc., 345 Hudson Street, New York, NY 10014. All rights reserved.

Philippa Pearce
"In the Middle of the Night." Copyright © 1972 Philippa Pearce from WHAT THE NEIGHBOURS DID AND OTHER STORIES (Puffin Books 1975) PERMISSION GRANTED BY THE AUTHOR.

Random House
"No One is Going to Nashville." Text copyright © 1983 by Mavis Jukes. Illustrations copyright © 1983 by Lloyd Bloom. Published by arrangement with Random House Children's Books, a division of Random House, Inc., New York New York. All rights reserved.

Scholastic, Inc.
"The Hope Bakery." From SOME OF THE KINDER PLANETS by Tim Wynne Jones. Published by Orchard Books/Scholastic Inc. Copyright © 1993 by Tim Wynne Jones. Reprinted by permission.

Simon & Schuster
"Why Bush Cow and Elephant are Bad Friends." Reprinted with the permission of Atheneum Books for Young Readers, an imprint of Simon & Schuster Children's Publishing Division from BEAT THE STORY-DRUM, PUM-PUM by Ashley Bryan. Copyright © 1980 Ashley Bryan.

Nancy Springer
"Barn Gravity" by Nancy Springer. Used by permission of the author.

Reading Mastery® is a registered trademark of the Mcgraw-Hill Companies

SRAonline.com

 SRA

Send all inquiries to this address:
SRA/McGraw-Hill
4400 Easton Commons
Columbus, OH 43219

ISBN: 978-0-07-612658-3
MHID: 0-07-612658-7

11 12 13 14 15 16 QVS 21 20 19 18 17

TABLE OF CONTENTS

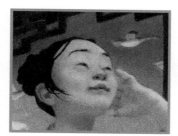

TABLE OF CONTENTS
continued

WHY BUSH COW AND ELEPHANT ARE BAD FRIENDS

Retold and illustrated by Ashley Bryan

New Vocabulary Words

1. dispute
2. slight
3. bout
4. clout, cuff
5. confer
6. limber up
7. lumber
8. havoc
9. bellow
10. verandah
11. praying mantis
12. grimace

Definitions

1. A **dispute** is an argument.
2. To **slight** someone is to treat that person as unimportant.
3. A **bout** is a fight.
4. During their bout, the animals exchanged **clouts** and **cuffs**; a **clout** is a blow and a **cuff** is a slap
5. When you **confer,** you talk about something important.
6. When you **limber up,** you stretch your body in ways that make it easier to bend and move.
7. To **lumber** is to walk heavily and noisily.
8. **Havoc** is another word for **destruction.**
9. When animals **bellow,** they roar.
10. A **verandah** is a covered porch attached to a building.
11. A **praying mantis** is an insect. When a **praying mantis** rests, it folds up its legs and looks like it is praying.
12. When you **grimace,** you twist up your face.

Story Background

Ashley Bryan is an African American writer and artist who was born in New York and lives in Maine. He has written and illustrated a number of books that contain his retellings of African folktales. "Why Bush Cow and Elephant Are Bad Friends" is a story that comes from one of these books.

When Ashley Bryan was a child, he read folktales and fairy tales from many countries. He also read novels, biographies, and poetry. But it was only when he was older that he found books about the accomplishments of black people. He believes that all American children should have the chance to read about people who were their ancestors, but that they should also read about people from other cultures.

When Ashley Bryan writes, he has fun with words. The first paragraph of "Why Bush Cow and Elephant Are Bad Friends" combines words that imitate the beats of a drum with words that introduce you to some of the main characters of the story. Words that imitate the sounds of a drum appear many times in the story. Read them out loud and make them sound like the beats of a drum.

You will have fun reading the words the monkey says out loud. The monkey speaks scat-talk. When jazz singers do scat singing, they sing a lot of repeated syllables to a melody. The syllables have no meaning. When you read the monkey's scat-talk, see if you can make it sound like scat singing.

As is true of folktales from many places in the world, "Why Bush Cow and Elephant Are Bad Friends" has some main characters that are animals and a main character who is a person. These characters are able to talk to each other. The elephant, the bush cow, the monkey, and the Head Chief have important conversations.

In his story, Ashley Bryan includes many details that describe life in African villages. Although the story takes place long ago, many of these details hold true today. For example, the Head Chief is still the most important person in a village. To make decisions, the Head Chief confers with the village elders. In many places in Africa, the people who live in the villages grow crops they sell in an open air market on market day.

The animals in the story "Why Bush Cow and Elephant Are Bad Friends" live in the bush. The word "bush" refers to the forest or jungle that surrounds a village. In this story, these two huge animals come out of the bush and have disputes that lead to fights that damage the fields of the people who live in the villages. The villagers don't like to have their fields ruined by these two huge animals. They turn to the Head Chief for help.

Focus Questions

- Why are the village elders so distraught when Bush Cow and Elephant have their disputes?
- What plans does the Head Chief make to resolve the first dispute between Bush Cow and Elephant? What happened to these plans?
- What does Monkey do that makes him such an important character?

WHY BUSH COW AND ELEPHANT ARE BAD FRIENDS

Retold and illustrated by Ashley Bryan

Beat the story-drum, *pum-pum!* Tell us a big story, *brum-brum!* The one about Elephant and Bush Cow, *thrum-thrum!* And of Monkey the messenger, *pittipong-pittipong!*

Bush Cow and Elephant were always bad friends. There was good reason why they didn't get along and could never settle their disputes.

Elephant was big, so was Bush Cow. They were nicknamed the Big Ones. They walked big, *brum-brum!* and talked big, *thrum-thrum!* It was the big, bad talk that got them into trouble, *pittipong-pittipong!*

Elephant liked to boast about his strength to everyone. He talked himself up and never missed making a slight or a put-down about Bush Cow's strength.

When Bush Cow heard that Elephant was bad-mouthing him, he felt ashamed and angry. He knew he was a good fighter and he feared no one. He told the tale-bearers a thing or two to take back to Elephant, *brum-brum!*

Wherever Bush Cow and Elephant walked, everyone stepped aside, no question about that. But because of the bad words that flew back and forth between them, neither Bush Cow nor Elephant would give way to the other. So whenever they met, they fought, *pum-pum!*

One day the Big Ones met on their way to market.

"Step aside and let me pass Bush Cow-ard," said Elephant, "or I'll braid your horns, *brum-brum!*"

"Out of my way, Snake Snout," said Bush Cow, "or I'll tie your trunk into knots, *thrum-thrum!*"

Greetings like that were bound to lead to blows. Elephant landed an opening clout; Bush Cow answered with a cuff; and then the bout was in full swing.

Bush Cow butted Elephant in his side. Elephant tripped Bush Cow with his trunk. They tumbled and tussled all over the field, pummeling each other as they rolled, *pum-pum! pum-pum!*

A crowd gathered. The village elders were distraught when they saw the torn-up field. They called out:

"Stop, stop! You're ruining the crop! Aie-yaie. It is as the proverb says: 'When two big ones fight, it is the grass that suffers.' Monkey, get closer and tell them to stop."

Monkey leaped into the tree nearest the fighters. He hung from the branches and chattered:

"Don't fee fa foo fight. It's not bee ba doo right."

Monkey's scat-talk was understood by everyone, but the Big Ones wouldn't listen to him. They kept on fighting.

Finally the Head Chief arrived and stopped the fight, for when the Head Chief commands, everyone obeys.

"What is happening here?" the Head Chief demanded.

Monkey hopped to him with his report:

"A fee fa foo fight. No bah ba dee body won. No nee na no noo, not one of the two. Not Bush Cow, I know. Not Elephant O. Wee why wo do they fight? What fee fa foo for? Their wee ba ree bop heads are hard as a door. It's always a draw."

"Door, draw!" said Elephant. "Suppose he hadn't stuck me with those horns, hah! I would have won, *thrum-thrum!*"

"Won, when!" said Bush Cow. "Suppose he hadn't tied my fists with his trunk, I would have flattened him, *brum-brum!*"

"Suppose, suppose," cried the Head Chief in disgust. "Suppose your head was a door post!"

Everyone laughed.

"But suppose," said the Big Ones, who were not laughing, "suppose we let you settle this dispute between us. We can't."

The Head Chief looked at the field and knew that something had to be done. He conferred with the village elders then announced the plan:

"Elephant and Bush Cow will meet to fight in the large open space of the marketplace next market day, *thrum-thrum!* This dispute will be settled then, once and for all, *brum-brum!* Everyone from country and town is invited to come and witness the battle, *pum-pum!*"

The Big Ones agreed, and all the details of the Battle of the Big Ones were settled. Then the villagers went on their way to the beat of the drums, *prum-prum, thrum-thrum, pum-pum, pittipong-pittipong!*

When market day of the fight dawned, Bush Cow rose early. He wanted to be the first one there to prove he was no coward. He limbered up quickly then lumbered along the main road. He heard that Elephant had not yet passed that way so he took up his position on the road to market at some distance from town.

Bush Cow blocked the road and waited. He became impatient and began bellowing and tearing up the ground, *brum-brum!*

"What have you done with Big Big One? Have you seen him? Where is he?" he cried to everyone who passed.

Monkey came along the road and was stopped and questioned.

"How should I na nee know of bee ba ba ray Big Big One?" said Monkey. "I'm a lee ba lu bay little monkey. But don't wa wu wait here. Sha ba dee boo no. Go on to the square. Chief a ree bop said oo soo bee doo fight there."

Bush Cow let Monkey pass, but he paid no attention to what he said. He stood right where he was. He stopped Doe, Zebra and Wild Boar with the same question before he heard Elephant trumpeting in the bush, *thrum-thrum!*

Elephant was breaking down trees and trampling the bushes in his way. That's how he kept in form for the fight. He came onto the main road to market. There stood Bush Cow, blocking the way.

"Move on to the square," said Elephant. "We agreed to fight there."

Bush Cow didn't like Elephant's tone of voice, so he stood his ground and glared at him.

"Move! Move Bush Cow-ard!" said Elephant.

"Move me then Snake Snout!" said Bush Cow.

"O me ma moo my," said Monkey. "Don't fee foo fight here. Move oo bee doo on to the square."

The Big Ones brushed Monkey aside. They didn't want to listen, and they didn't waste words. They lowered their heads and charged, *powf!* That was the end of their promise to fight in the marketplace.

A tremendous battle began. The Big Ones pitched, rolled and tossed, damaging the nearby farms. The villagers were frightened from going on to market and hid out of harm's way, hoping the havoc would soon halt. The village elders were shocked when they came on the scene. They couldn't believe the Big Ones would disobey the Head Chief's battle plan.

"Monkey," they said, "quick! Run and tell the Head Chief all that is happening here."

Monkey had watched the fight from the start so he knew the message. He set off quickly, swinging through the branches and squealing as he swung. When he stopped a moment to catch his breath, he could no longer remember why he was in such a hurry, where he was going and what he was to say to whom, which is the forgetful way that monkeys have.

"Now why, where, to who, what for?" he asked himself. "What, where, why, to who? Shoo bee do, shoo bee do!"

Monkey danced, "Hay baa ba ree bop, hay baa..." Suddenly the message sprang back into his mind.

"Skoo bee do, skoo bee do," he sang in delight. He went on as fast as he could go so that he would not forget the message again.

When Monkey reached the Head Chief's house he remembered, "Shoo bee do" and "skoo bee do," but nothing more. He hadn't the slightest idea why he had come.

Well, he had arrived and that was something. He could at least act as if he were about important business. Shoo bee do, shoo bee do! he'd look busy, yeah!

Monkey sat down and engaged in a minute personal inspection of his fur. A minute later whop! he jumped up onto the roof of the house, *pittipong-pittipong!* He caught and ate a bug, then down he swung again to the ground.

There he found a stone and he rolled it around, backward and forward, forward and back, in an aimless sort of way while looking in the opposite direction.

Monkey soon tired of this and picked up a stick. He tapped out a rhythm on the stone, *whick, whack-a-whack; whick, whack-a-crack!* the stick broke. He flung the pieces into the bushes and flung the stone after them.

Monkey hopped onto the verandah and crouched with his head in his hands. He was almost at wit's end when his attention was attracted by a large praying mantis that fluttered past him into the Head Chief's house. It circled the room with a loud clatter of wings then settled on the floor and immediately assumed its usual prayerful attitude.

Monkey stalked the mantis carefully and was just about to seize it when the chief caught sight of him and shouted out in a loud voice:

"Ha, Monkey, is that you?"

At the sound of the Head Chief's voice, Monkey did a back flip and mantis flapped out the front door.

"Who, who?" cried Monkey. "O ya you no me. Yes-siree, it's bee ba dee me."

"What brings you here?" asked the chief.

"To see shoo bee do you. Yeah!"

Monkey cocked his head to one side, trying to look as if he had something wise to add to that. Actually he was thinking of nothing. He began chattering nervously about sticks and stones and mantis bones because everything else had gone out of his head, *pittipong-pittipong!*

"Well" said the Head Chief "if you've nothing more on your mind than that, then help yourself to one of the ripe bananas hanging up in the verandah."

Monkey was very fond of bananas and didn't need to be told twice. He went quickly and chose a large one, then returned to the room. Monkey peeled the banana and bit first one end, then the other, as if that would make it last longer. He studied the banana carefully after each bite.

"Monkey," said the Head Chief, "shouldn't Bush Cow and Elephant be here by now? I've been waiting for them all morning. They promised to meet in the market square for the big battle today."

Yoweee! Monkey somersaulted and came down chattering: "O sure shoo bee do, sure, sure shoo bee do!"

Monkey swallowed the last bit of banana, and after all sorts of scat-talk, squeals and grimaces told the Head Chief all of the elder's message.

"Aha!" said the Head Chief, "so that's why the market is almost empty today. Thanks for the message, Monkey. Help yourself to another banana. As for Bush Cow and Elephant, I'll see to it that they get theirs, *thrum-thrum!*"

Monkey ate the banana, pleased and impressed with himself. He was sure that there were not many others who could manage a message to match his style, shoo bee do, shoo bee do!

The Head Chief called for his bow and arrows, and Monkey led him to the scene of the battle. When the Head Chief arrived and saw the ruined farmlands, he didn't ask questions and he didn't raise his voice. Instead, he raised his arm with the bow and shot first one arrow, then another, *plung, plung!*

Bush Cow felt a sharp stab in his rump, *wow!*

Elephant felt a sharp stab in his rump, *wow!*

The Head Chief didn't wait. He shot a second volley of arrows and prepared to shoot a third.

But Bush Cow and Elephant got the message. They didn't wait for any more arrows to fly. They flew! They plunged into the bush and disappeared, *brum-brum!*

After that the Head Chief refused to have anything more to do with settling disputes between Bush Cow and Elephant. But ever since then, when wild animals fight, they always fight in the bush and not on public roads, *thrum-thrum!*

Since the big battle between Bush Cow and Elephant was never decided, each still boasts that he is the stronger. Whenever they meet along main roads, they argue. Whenever they meet in the bush, they fight.

So to this day, *pum-pum!* Bush Cow and Elephant, *thrum-thrum!* remain bad friends, *brum-brum!*

Pittipong-pittipong!

Extending Comprehension

Story Questions

1. Who stops the first fight between Bush Cow and Elephant? Who isn't able to stop that fight?
2. Why are the villagers distraught?
3. After he confers with the village elders, the Head Chief announces his plan. Describe the plan.
4. Why doesn't the Head Chief's plan work?
5. Why does it take so long for Monkey to get the message about the tremendous battle to the Head Chief?
6. How does the Head Chief punish Bush Cow and Elephant?
7. What do all of the other wild animals learn?
8. What happens when Bush Cow and Elephant meet along the main roads?
9. What happens when they meet in the bush?

Discussion Topics

1. Bush Cow and Elephant are big and very strong. They insult each other and then have a fight. The Head Chief tries to resolve their dispute by planning a time and place for them to have the fight that he thinks will settle their problems. Can you think of other ways that the problems between the two animals could be resolved? During your discussion, try to answer the following questions:

   • Why are Bush Cow and Elephant such bad friends?

   • What are some different plans the Head Chief might have suggested?

   • Do you think there is any chance of Bush Cow and Elephant ever becoming good friends?

2. The author uses a lot of vivid language to describe how Bush Cow and Elephant insult each other. He uses even more vivid language to describe the noises these big animals make when they fight. Can you come up with some additional language that would make the story even better?

   During your discussion, look back in the story to answer some of the following questions:

   • What are some examples from the story of how Bush Cow and Elephant insult each other?

   • What are some examples of the words used to describe the noises Bush Cow and Elephant make as they walk though the bush, talk to each other, and fight with each other?

   • Can you think of other words that would help readers get an even better picture of how Bush Cow and Elephant feel about each other?

3. The first time Bush Cow and Elephant fight, the village elders call out: "Stop, stop! ...It is as the proverb says: 'When two big ones fight, it is the grass that suffers.'" A proverb is a statement that expresses a well-known truth or fact. Discuss the meaning of this proverb. During your discussion, try to answer the following questions:

   • How does this proverb describe what is happening in the story?

   • In what other situations could the proverb be used?

1. Monkey runs to tell the Head Chief that the Big Ones have started their fight. Start with what happened when Monkey reaches the Head Chief's house and make a list of all of the things Monkey does before he finally gives the Head Chief the message. Then write a paragraph that summarizes your conclusions about the usefulness of Monkey as a messenger.

2. "Why Bush Cow and Elephant Are Bad Friends" is one story that explains why wild animals in Africa no longer fight on public roads, but instead fight in the bush. Other stories could give a different explanation. Make up another story that explains why wild animals do not fight on public roads.

3. Pretend you are Monkey. Write a description of the scene in which the Head Chief punishes Bush Cow and Elephant. You must sound like Monkey when you write your description. Don't forget to use some scat-talk.

BLUE WILLOW

by Pam Conrad
Illustrated by S. Saelig Gallagher

New Vocabulary Words

1. merchant
2. scroll
3. pavilion

4. embroider
5. lute
6. reluctance

7. turmoil
8. topple
9. commission
10. heed

Definitions

1. A **merchant** is a person who buys and sells things.
2. A **scroll** is a long piece of fine paper or silk that people write on. A scroll is rolled up when not in use.
3. A **pavilion** is an open building where you can sit to watch a performance or observe nature.
4. When you **embroider,** you sew designs on a cloth.
5. A **lute** is a stringed musical instrument that has an egg-shaped guitar body with the neck bent back.

6. When you do something with **reluctance,** you do it unwillingly and without enthusiasm.
7. **Turmoil** is another way of saying *chaos and confusion.*
8. When things or people **topple,** they fall over.
9. When you **commission** a piece of art, you pay the artist to make the piece of art the way you want it designed.
10. When you **heed** what someone tells you, you pay attention and listen to what is said.

Story Background

"Blue Willow" is Pam Conrad's personal interpretation of a Chinese legend. She learned about the legend from a Blue Willow plate that was in her family. Blue Willow plates were first made in England during the 1700s, when British culture was greatly influenced by Chinese culture. The pattern on the plates became very popular in England and America. Blue Willow plates are still made and collected today. The legend was inspired by the beautiful pattern. As

is typical of legends, there are many versions, but the basic ingredients remain the same.

Pam Conrad wrote her version of the Blue Willow legend when her daughter grew up and fell in love. Pam Conrad's message is one for all parents: Listen to your children and take them seriously when they speak to you about matters of the heart.

Much of this legend takes place outdoors. Here are some words particular to this setting that will help you understand and enjoy the story. **Peonies** and **orchids** are flowers known for their beautiful blossoms. **Cassias** and **willows** are types of trees. **Sandpipers** and **cormorants** are birds that are found near water. **Cicadas** are insects that make loud, shrill sounds.

Water plays an important role in this legend. **Monsoons** are seasonal winds that bring very heavy rains that often result in flooding. **Monsoon rains** can be described as **torrential** because so much water comes down. Other words that describe this intense movement of water are **surging** and **churning.**

Jewelry also has a part in this legend. Since Kung Shi Fair is the daughter of a wealthy man, she is used to the finest jewelry made of gold. Gold can be described as **lustrous** because of its luster, or shiny quality. **Trinkets** are cheap jewelry of little or no monetary value. For Kung Shi Fair, trinkets are made of **jade,** a green-colored mineral; of **ivory,** from animal tusks; or of **brass,** an inexpensive metal.

Chang the Good, the young man whom Kung Shi Fair wants to marry, brings her a variety of trinkets as a sign of his affection. To Chang, these are his most precious treasures, as they had belonged to his mother, who died when he was young. In a simple bundle, he brings necklaces, pendants (necklaces with jewels hanging from them), and bracelets, along with brooches to pin on Kung Shi Fair's clothing.

Focus Questions

- Why is Kung Shi Fair's father reluctant to give his daughter the one thing she wants from him?
- Because they love each other, what do Kung Shi Fair and Chang the Good do during the raging storm?
- What lesson does the wealthy merchant learn, and what does he do so others might benefit from his mistakes?

BLUE WILLOW

Written by Pam Conrad ‡ Illustrated by S. Saelig Gallagher

Many years ago, long before you were born, there was a river called Wen that flowed through the mountains, over the countryside, and past a small and peaceful village.

On one side of the Wen River, in a large mansion with rich and glorious gardens, lived a wealthy merchant. He had no friends. He hardly walked in his gardens, played no musical instrument, but he knew the number and weight of all he possessed— every grain of rice, every newborn dove, and every candle that melted away was recorded by his pointed brush on fine scrolls.

Everyone knew that he had one daughter, Kung Shi Fair, and that because his wife was dead, he treasured this daughter more than all his possessions. And it was thought by all that she was a girl who deserved such love.

Kung Shi Fair was a beautiful girl with hands as small as starfish, feet as swift as sandpipers, and hair as black as the ink on her father's scrolls. As she grew, the people of the village waited and wondered who she would marry, because they all knew that the merchant always gave her whatever she asked for.

Once she had said, "Father, I would have a moon pavilion of my very own," and he built one for her to sit in and paint her pictures. It was surrounded by peonies that filled the air with sweetness, and bamboo that sounded like wings beating in the wind.

Another day she said, "Father, I would have a boat made of cassia with fig leaf sails and a banner of orchids." And this too he had made for her, but because he loved her so much, he would not let her put it in the water.

Another time she said, "Father, I would have a stone bridge of my very own," and beneath the willow tree he built her a footbridge that led to her moon pavilion.

The favorite story of the villagers was how one day she had even said, "Father, I would like some small green frogs to waken in the morning when I cross my very own bridge," and he sent his two servants to find small green frogs and place them beneath the bridge.

*T*he villagers watched from the other side of the river. They were not wealthy like the merchant, neither were they poor. They were hardworking people who knew how to plow a rice field with a tired ox, and how to embroider golden dragons on silk robes with short pieces of yellow thread. They were good people who loved to see Kung Shi Fair sitting in her pavilion. Sometimes the village children would wave to her, but Kung Shi Fair would look away.

*O*ne day Kung Shi Fair was sitting in her moon pavilion when she saw something glistening on the bank of the river. She abandoned her paintbrush and carefully made her way through the bamboo and peonies to the water. When she got there, she saw it was only a broken shell. She picked it up and turned it over in her hands, then looked up and saw for the first time a boat and a young man pulling his dripping nets out of the water.

This was Chang the Good who lived across the river. He was a young fisherman who counted his wealth in nets and cormorants and the slant of the wind across the river's surface. He was a strong boy with a good heart, and the village people said of him that if in the darkness of a monsoon night you were to reach out and feel warmth beneath your hand, you would say, "Is this the shank of a hardy ox, or is this the long back of Chang the Good?" He was that strong and that steady. And that well loved.

Now Kung Shi Fair and Chang the Good were both startled to see each other. The fish spilled out of his nets, and the cormorant flapped unheeded in the air. Some say there was even the sound of bells tinkling in the slow drift of the river. The shell dropped from Kung Shi Fair's hand, and tossing the nets on the floor of his boat, Chang the Good picked up his oars, and never taking his eyes off Kung Shi Fair, he rowed across the river to her.

When he reached the shore, Kung Shi Fair watched as he pulled the boat onto the land. She came close and touched his nets. "How beautiful," she said. "I have never seen nets this close."

"I made them myself," he told her, thinking he, as well, had never seen something so beautiful this close.

"And what a wonderful bird!" she exclaimed as the cormorant held out its wings to dry in the breeze.

"I fish with her. She dives for fish because of the ring around her neck—and because I have trained her so well— she brings the fish to me."

"You are very clever," she said, turning her gaze full on him. The same wind that rustled her lavender silk robe tugged at his coarse, river-wet shirt. The same sand touched their feet. The same sun shone on both their heads.

"Can I tell you something?" he asked her softly.

She nodded, silent.

"One morning I came down to the river, thinking my boat would be anchored where I had left it, but it had gotten loose in the night, and the currents had taken it away. All day long I searched along the river for my boat and could not find it. Then toward evening, when I had given up hope, I came upon a still cove, and there it was, drifting toward me. My heart swelled with love."

Kung Shi Fair tilted her head. "And so?"

"And so, this is how I felt just now, seeing you here on the bank of the river."

Kung Shi Fair frowned. "My boat has never been in the river," she said. "So I have never lost a boat, or found one." Then she smiled at him. "But I came to the river just now thinking I saw something glistening on its bank, and now I know I came for you."

Kung Shi Fair and Chang the Good were alone on the shore of the Wen River, but the people of the village have told this story ever since. This was the beginning of the story, the good, the happy part.

But it so happened that Kung Shi Fair's father was watching from the window of his mansion. His hand was tired from writing his lists, and he had risen to stretch his legs. He watched as his daughter led the fisherman across the stone foot bridge, where their footsteps woke the sleeping frogs, and he watched her lead Chang the Good to her moon pavilion.

*T*hat night he said nothing to his daughter about what he had seen. But he watched her and saw how her cheeks were high with color and how her smile came so easily. He noticed a new tenderness about her, how she touched even the flowers on the table with great care.

They were drinking their tea, sitting quietly and listening to the late summer cicadas, when one of the servants came panting onto the veranda.

"There is terrible news, Master, from down the river. It seems there is a wild leopard on a rampage. It is tearing down small houses and killing people."

"This is frightening," the merchant said. "You must tell me if you hear news of the leopard coming in this direction."

"Yes, Master," the servant answered, and he backed out of the room.

The merchant looked at his daughter. "Perhaps, until the leopard is caught, you should stay near the house and not go down into your moon pavilion."

Kung Shi Fair clapped her hands and laughed. "Don't be silly, silly father. My pavilion is perfectly safe." Then she took down her lute and played some of his favorite songs so that he would forget about the leopard…and about her pavilion.

*T*he next day and every day after that, when the work of fishing was through, Kung Shi Fair and Chang the Good would meet on the shore. First they would go to the pavilion, where the silk-lined ceilings and walls rustled, and long-legged, pale green insects would watch them. Then they would trail peony petals down the path to the bridge, where they would sit and talk, and eat mulberries beneath the cool willow tree.

Finally, after many days of this, Chang the Good came with a bundle. It was a red silk bundle tied in a fisherman's knot. Without speaking, he led her over the bridge and into her pavilion.

"I have something to show you," he said. "Sit down," and she did.

Very carefully, in the late afternoon sun, he unfastened the knot and opened his bundle on the floor before her. There were jade brooches and ivory necklaces, brass bracelets, and pendants hung not on gold chains as she was used to, but on rough silk cords dull with wear.

Not knowing Kung Shi Fair had more jewelry than she could ever wear, Chang the Good held up a necklace spread in his fingers, and she bowed her head and allowed him to place it around her neck. Then another necklace and another, weighing her down. He slipped a bracelet over her small hand, and another and another. Kung Shi Fair grew quiet and still, studying his face.

He told her, "These belonged to my mother, who died when I was very young."

Now Kung Shi Fair was a rich girl, used to precious jewels and lustrous gold, and she did not know what to say about the humble pile of trinkets that Chang the Good offered her. But she could see that to Chang the Good these were great treasures, all the riches he owned. So now, with the heart of someone who has learned to love, she knew that these were the most precious gifts she had ever received.

"And this was her own ring," Chang the Good was saying, and he slipped a small jade ring onto her thumb.

"Beautiful," Kung Shi Fair told him, and she truly meant it. "I have never seen anything more beautiful."

"I want you to have them," he told her. "I want you to be my wife."

Kung Shi Fair held very still. The silk on the walls and the ceiling floated in the air. The long-legged, green bugs listened. The bamboo sounded like wings beating in the wind.

"Yes, I would like this, too," she said. "But I must tell my father." And she began taking off all the necklaces and bracelets.

"Keep them," he begged. "I want you to have them."

"No, no. I cannot," she said. "Not yet. Not until I am your wife."

But Chang the Good's hand folded over hers. "Keep the ring at least. Keep the ring in good faith until we can marry." And she agreed.

That night Kung Shi Fair went to her father, the father who had built her a moon pavilion and a boat when she asked, the very father who had built her a stone bridge when she wanted one, and the same father who had sent out servants to collect frogs for her. Knowing now that all those things were no longer what she truly wanted, she said to him, "I would marry now, Father."

And he answered, "Not yet, my daughter, not yet."

At that moment, a servant ran into the room.

"There is more news, Master, from down the river. The wild leopard is coming closer. It has killed more people. It leaves death everywhere."

"This is terrible," the merchant said. "Find out how close the leopard is."

"Yes, Master," the servant answered, and he backed out of the room.

Kung Shi Fair had barely heard the servant. "But, Father, you have always been so good to me. And this is what I want more than anything. If not now, then when?"

The merchant ran his hand over the top of his head and stared sadly out the window. "When the first call of the migrant geese is heard over the land, when the cicadas are still. And maybe you should stay away from your pavilion for a while."

"Oh, Father," she sighed, but he held up his hand and would hear no more.

*K*ung Shi Fair could not get married without her father's permission, but she did not stay away from her moon pavilion. Chang the Good was not discouraged by the news of her father's reluctance. One day when he was leaving, he told her, "Summer is nearly over, so we will wait for the migrating geese."

Laughing and turning his boat out into the gentle current, he promised to crush beneath his foot every cicada he could find until there was not a single one left. Kung Shi Fair stood on the shore and watched him sail away. Across the river, for the first time, she saw the village children waving to her, and feeling hopeful, she waved back.

*A*utumn came quickly that year, bringing sudden cool evenings and a fast churning river. Kung Shi Fair was having dinner with her father one night when she heard a distant honking. She leapt to her feet. "Father! Father! Come out on the terrace," and he, knowing, hearing the geese himself, reluctantly walked out beside her. They stood together, heads back, and watched the geese fly overhead.

"Now?" she whispered. "Now can I be married?"

"Not yet, my daughter, not yet."

She stared at him in disbelief. "Then when?"

"When I find a copper coin in my path," he said.

"Oh, Father, that is not fair. How will I know if you find a copper coin in your path? You will keep it from me!"

But at this her father held up his hands to silence her. "Enough!" he shouted, and he turned away.

With the sound of the honking geese still ringing in her ears, Kung Shi Fair ran from the room to hide her tears, past the servant who was coming to tell the merchant that the leopard was terribly close.

*C*hang the Good could not be discouraged. Sitting in Kung Shi Fair's moon pavilion, he thought of a plan. He did not stay that day for he had special work to do, and he told Kung Shi Fair to sit by her window at dawn.

The next morning, Kung Shi Fair watched the rain paint little jewels on her hands as she leaned on the window. Her father was preparing to go to a village meeting concerning the rampaging leopard. She saw the servants bring the carriage around to him, and just as her father was about to climb on, he looked down and saw coins strewn at his feet—hundreds of little copper coins. He looked up at his daughter in the window.

She saw no anger in his face, just sadness. She smiled kindly at him. "Now, Father? Can I now?"

He shook his head. "Not yet, my daughter, not yet."

Her smile turned to tears that mingled with the rain. "Then when, Father? Oh, then when?"

"When there's a rainbow over the stone bridge that leads to your moon pavilion," he told her, and he drove away.

*L*ater the servants claimed to have heard Kung Shi Fair's sad crying that morning, even above winds that whistled over the river's surface. They told how Kung Shi Fair was brokenhearted, and that it was more than she could bear. They decided she had gone to find Chang the Good, to tell him his plan had failed.

The village women later whispered about how she went down to the bank of the tumbling Wen River, to her boat that had never been wet. She had watched many times as Chang the Good had pushed off the bank and sailed away, and now—hoping she could remember how, just from watching—she awkwardly pushed her boat of cassia, fig leaves, and orchid banners into the surging river.

Turning her young and determined face into the wind, she steered bravely through the river's foam and rapids. She rode the river's swells and currents. But this is the sad part of the story, and perhaps the worst part, because when she was halfway across the river, the wind ripped the fig leaf sails from their mast, and the orchids were torn and bruised, and the cassia bark hull snapped apart, tipping the merchant's beautiful daughter into the torrential river. For a few moments her silken robe could be seen floating near the surface, and then it was gone.

In the village, knowing there would be a storm, Chang the Good had not gone down to his boat that morning. Instead he had gone to the village meeting to hear the news about the rampaging leopard. Everyone was in great turmoil, frightened that the leopard would come right into their village and kill their families. Chang the Good noticed that Kung Shi Fair's father was there, and he smiled to himself thinking of all the coins the merchant must have found at his feet that morning. But Chang the Good did not speak. In time, he was sure Kung Shi Fair would present him to her father, so he stayed at the back of the hall and listened. The villagers were clearly upset, wringing their hands and crying. Then the merchant spoke to them.

"While the storm is raging," he said, "we must go out, seek the leopard, and slay him before he comes to our village and kills again."

"Yes!" "Yes!" the villagers cried. "We will find the leopard before he finds us!" "Kill the leopard now!"

Chang the Good had thoughts only for Kung Shi Fair. He had no heart for a hunt. Without being seen, he stepped out into the rain, walked slowly to stand beneath a pear tree, and turned his eyes to the river. He thought to himself how once the rain stopped and the winds calmed, he would sail over and see her and ask her how things had gone with her father and the coins.

Meanwhile the swords were brought out and the bows and arrows, the spears and the clubs, and everyone received a weapon. The villagers poured out of the hall, out of every house and temple, and they took to the rain-slick road, in search of the leopard.

*I*t was dark when the winds finally calmed and the river slowed its fury. Out of habit, the cormorant perched on the back of Chang the Good's boat, as he eased it into the river. Chang the Good gave it a final push and jumped in. Slowly and carefully, he made his way across, peering into the darkness of the pavilion to see if Kung Shi Fair waited for him. But there was no sign of her.

He pulled his boat ashore and called, "Kung Shi!" There was silence.

He ran up the shore and to the bridge, the cormorant flapping behind him. "Kung Shi!"

He ran to the pavilion and threw back the rain-soaked silks. "Kung Shi!"

Frightened, he turned toward her father's house that was dark and lifeless. His feet barely touched the ground. The cormorant shrieked and swooped after him. At the threshold of the house, he called again, and when there was no answer, he entered. He ran from room to room, calling her name and hearing the silence answer. He knew something terrible had happened. But he did not know what it was.

Slowly he left the house. The song of the small green frogs carried him to the stone bridge and he decided to sit there and wait for her. Surely she would come back to him soon. She would walk across this bridge and find him. He sat silently with the cormorant beside him, her black wings spread. The moon slipped out of the clouds and hung in the willow, polishing the water beneath his dangling feet.

Suddenly the cormorant flapped her wings and shrieked. She peered into the water. "Not now," Chang the Good told her. "Tomorrow we work."

But she did not listen to him. Before he could stop her, the cormorant dived into the water and disappeared into the shimmering darkness. Then in a spray of water she flew straight up and landed beside Chang the Good. She was not obliged to turn over her catch, but she dropped what she was carrying into her master's hand.

It was a small, jade thumb ring.

Chang the Good saw it and at that moment, he knew. He jumped up, and his eyes searched the shore for the cassia boat with the fig leaf sails and the orchid banners and he knew. He saw the whole story before him and threw back his head. He knew it was too late.

Just as the moon began to slip into sight, the weary villagers were returning home empty-handed. They were uneasy with the hunt, anxious to be back with their children and their oxen, their wives and their homes. There had been no leopard to kill, no prey for their hunt. They mumbled that perhaps it had all been a rumor.

As they came back toward the village, they heard a sound coming from across the water near the merchant's house. "The leopard!" they whispered, fingering their spears. "We must kill him!" At that, three of them jumped into a boat and sailed silently across the river to the place where the sound came from.

Now for many years after, the villagers tried to describe to each other what the sound was like. Some said it was a lonely wailing. Others said it was like the sound of a trapped animal just before it dies. Most thought it sounded like the ragings of a rampaging leopard before it strikes. Later they all knew it was the sound of Chang the Good, crying his heart into the night.

Silently the boat slipped onto the river bank, and the three men crept up the shore. In the moonlight they saw their enemy. On the bridge, in the silver reflection of the river they saw a leopard with savage teeth and murderous claws. In one thrust they all shot arrows, threw spears, and sent clubs sailing through the wailing air. Their mark was made, and Chang the Good toppled into the river beneath the bridge.

If this was the end of the story, it would probably have been forgotten by now, it was so long ago. But because the merchant was so heartbroken, he cried his sorrows to whomever would listen to him, and the entire village soon knew he had kept his daughter away from the man she loved by demanding a rainbow over the stone bridge that led to her moon pavilion.

It was some time later, while the last leaves were still on the willow, turning yellow from cool evenings, that there was a cloudburst in the late afternoon. The merchant was at his scrolls, writing with black ink and an empty heart, when he heard the villagers cry out on the opposite shore of the river, and he went to the window.

His heart leapt at the sight, for just above the foot
bridge that led to his daughter's pavilion, there appeared
a most wondrous rainbow of every color, and while the
villagers watched, and while the merchant watched, two
swallows fluttered above the willow tree and kissed, their
wings making the sound of wind in bamboo.

In order that this story never be forgotten, the merchant commissioned a plate be made to tell the story. The village artist, who had known Chang the Good and loved him like a brother, did a fine painting of the merchant's mansion, the village across the river, Chang the Good's boat, the moon pavilion, and the three hunters on the bridge. He did not paint a leopard, for after the storm no one ever heard of the leopard again, and many wondered if it had existed at all.

But over the willow tree he placed the two swallows in flight at the moment they kissed. Around them he tried to paint a border of what the rainbow had looked like, and around that border another border with the designs that had been on the simple jewelry that Chang the Good had offered to Kung Shi Fair.

When the plates were finished, the merchant gave them to everyone in the village and anyone who came through the village. He said he did it so that parents everywhere would always listen to their children, and would always, always heed what was in their children's hearts.

Extending Comprehension

Story Questions

1. In what ways does Kung Shi Fair's father spoil her?
2. Where and how do Chang and Kung Shi Fair meet?
3. What is the terrible news delivered by one of the merchant's servants?
4. What are the different ways the merchant puts off his daughter's most important request?
5. How does Chang react to the merchant's reluctance?
6. What do the villagers decide to do, in spite of the raging storm?
7. Why doesn't Chang join the villagers? Where does he go instead?
8. What does Chang realize when his cormorant brings him something other than a fish from the water?
9. Where does Kung Shi Fair go during the storm and why?
10. After almost giving up on finding the leopard, the villagers hear a sound. What happens next?
11. What do the villagers later figure out about the sound?
12. What does the merchant do so his daughter and Chang the Good are never forgotten?
13. What lesson does the merchant learn?

Discussion Topics

1. Do you think there was a leopard rampaging through the village? How might the legend be different if there hadn't been a leopard? During your discussion, try to answer the following questions:

   - Why do you think a leopard is included as part of the legend?

   - What evidence suggests there was a leopard?

   - What evidence suggests there might not have been a leopard?

2. Water is like a character in this legend. What are some of the important roles that water plays? During your discussion, try to answer the following questions:

   - What different events take place on the river?

   - What happens because of the torrential rains?

   - Could there have been a rainbow over the stone bridge without water?

3. This legend has a tragic ending. How could the deaths of the main characters have been avoided? During your discussion, try to answer the following questions:

   - Why didn't Kung Shi Fair know how to use her boat?

   - Why didn't Chang the Good go on the leopard hunt with the other villagers?

   - How are the three villagers feeling as they jump into their boats to go kill the leopard?

   - If Kung Shi Fair's father had agreed to let his daughter marry Chang the Good, would the couple have behaved differently the night of the storm?

4. If you have access to the Internet, go to the following Web site: www.willowcollectors.org/legends.html. On the Web site, there is a poem about the Blue Willow legend. Read it aloud. Discuss the similarities and differences between the poem and the story you read.

Writing Ideas

1. Chang is a clever young man. For example, he trains his cormorant to bring fish back to him. Write a letter to Kung Shi Fair's father explaining why Chang is a worthy husband for his daughter.

2. The author uses figurative language, specifically similes, to describe the sound Chang makes when he learns of Kung Shi's death. These examples include: "like the sound of a trapped animal just before it dies" and "like the ragings of a rampaging leopard before it strikes."

   Try to imagine the sound Chang made at that terrible moment and write two of your own similes to describe what you hear. Then try to imagine Kung Shi's fear and horror as the hull of her boat snapped apart and she was pulled into the surging river. Write two more similes to describe Kung Shi's feelings.

3. A famous saying states that, "Money can't buy happiness." Why is the Blue Willow legend a good example of what that saying means? Write a paragraph that explains your answer. Be sure to answer the following questions:

   - Which characters have a lot of money? Are they happy?

   - Which characters do not have a lot of money? Are they happy?

   - What is the one thing Kung Shi Fair wants that her father can't buy for her?

In the Middle of the Night

by Philippa Pearce
Illustrated by Mike Zirbes

New Vocabulary Words

1. alight
2. suffocate
3. dislodge

4. upheaval
5. obstruction
6. larder

7. methodical
8. aghast
9. paradise

Definitions

1. When something **alights,** it descends and settles in one place.
2. When you can't get enough air to breathe, you **suffocate.**
3. When you **dislodge** something, you remove or force it out of a particular place.
4. An **upheaval** is a disruption or a disturbance.
5. An **obstruction** is something that gets in your way.
6. A **larder** is a cupboard or a room for storing food. Some people call a larder a pantry.
7. When you do things in a **methodical** way, you do them in an orderly and precise way.
8. When you are **aghast** at something, that thing horrifies and amazes you.
9. **Paradise** is a wonderful, happy place.

Story Background

Philippa Pearce is a British author of children's books. She writes for newspapers and radio and is also a storyteller. "In the Middle of the Night" is a funny story about what happens when a boy named Charlie is awakened during the night. There are many clues in this story that let you know the author is not American. Below are some of the expressions and words she uses. See if you can figure out what they mean.

1. She covered his mouth and said, "Don't **make a row** or you'll wake up the whole family!" What do you think **make a row** means?

2. Before you go out in the rain, you better put on a raincoat, your boots, and your **sou'wester** on your head. What piece of clothing is a sou'wester?

3. On Sundays, Mum always made us eat a **proper breakfast.** What would a proper breakfast be?

4. The young child curled up in her bed and her mom covered her with a soft and cozy **eiderdown.** What do you think an eiderdown is?

In the Middle of the Night

by Philippa Pearce
Illustrated by Mike Zirbes

Focus Questions

- How and why do the older children trick their younger brother, Wilson?
- How and why does Alison trick her mother?

In the middle of the night a fly woke Charlie. At first he lay listening, half-asleep, while it swooped about the room. Sometimes it was far; sometimes it was near—that was what had woken him; and occasionally it was very near indeed. It was very, very near when the buzzing stopped; the fly had alighted on his face. He jerked his head up; the fly buzzed off. Now he was really awake.

The fly buzzed widely about the room, but it was thinking of Charlie all the time. It swooped nearer and nearer. Nearer....

Charlie pulled his head down under the bedclothes. All of him under the bedclothes, he was completely protected; but he could hear nothing except his heartbeats and his breathing. He was overwhelmed by the smell of warm bedding, warm pajamas, warm himself. He was going to suffocate. So he rose suddenly up out of the bedclothes; and the fly was waiting for him. It dashed at him. He beat at it with his hands. At the same time he appealed to his younger brother, Wilson, in the next bed: "Wilson, there's a fly!"

Wilson, unstirring, slept on.

Now Charlie and the fly were pitting their wits against each other: Charlie pouncing on the air where he thought the fly must be; the fly sliding under his guard towards his face. Again and again the fly reached Charlie; again and again, almost simultaneously, Charlie dislodged him. Once he hit the fly—or, at least, hit where the fly had been a second before, on the side of his head; the blow so hard that his head sang with it afterwards.

Then suddenly the fight was over; no more buzzing. His blows—or rather, one of them—must have told.

He laid his head back on the pillow, thinking of going to sleep again. But he was also thinking of the fly, and now he noticed a tickling in the ear he turned to the pillow.

It must be—it *was*—the fly.

He rose in such panic that the waking of Wilson really seemed to him a possible thing, and useful. He shook him repeatedly. "Wilson, Wilson, I tell you, there's a fly in my ear!"

Wilson groaned, turned over slowly like a seal in water, and slept on.

The tickling in Charlie's ear continued. He could just imagine the fly struggling in some passageway too narrow for its wingspan. He longed to put his finger into his ear and rattle it around, like a stick in a rabbit hole; but he was afraid of driving the fly deeper into his ear.

Wilson slept on.

Charlie stood in the middle of the bedroom floor, quivering and trying to think. He needed to see down his ear, or to get someone else to see down it. Wilson wouldn't do; perhaps Margaret would.

Margaret's room was next door. Charlie turned on the light as he entered: Margaret's bed was empty. He was startled, and then thought that she must have gone to the bathroom. But there was no light from there. He listened carefully: there was no sound from anywhere, except for the usual snuffling moans from the hall, where Floss slept and dreamed of dog biscuits. The empty bed was mystifying; but Charlie had his ear to worry about. It sounded as if there were a pigeon inside it now.

Wilson asleep; Margaret vanished; that left Alison. But Alison was bossy, just because she was the eldest; and anyway she would probably only wake Mum. He might as well wake Mum himself.

Down the passage and through the door always left ajar. "Mum," he said. She woke, or at least half-woke, at once. "Who is it? Who? Who? What's the matter? What? —"

"I've a fly in my ear."

"You can't have."

"It flew in."

She switched on the bedside light, and as she did so, Dad plunged beneath the bedclothes with an exclamation and lay still again.

Charlie knelt at his mother's side of the bed, and she looked into his ear. "There's nothing."

"Something crackles."

"It's wax in your ear."

"It tickles."

"There's no fly there. Go back to bed and stop imagining things."

His father's arm came up from below the bedclothes. The hand waved about, settled on the bedside light, and clicked it out. There was an upheaval of bedclothes and a comfortable grunt.

"Good night," said Mum from the darkness. She was already allowing herself to sink back into sleep again.

"Good night," Charlie said sadly. Then an idea occurred to him. He repeated his good night loudly and added some coughing, to cover the fact that he was closing the bedroom door behind him—the door that Mum kept open so that she could listen for her children. They had outgrown all that kind of attention, except possibly for Wilson. Charlie had shut the door against Mum's hearing because he intended to slip downstairs for a drink of water—well, for a drink and perhaps a snack. That fly business had woken him up and also weakened him; he needed something.

He crept downstairs, trusting to Floss's good sense not to make a row. He turned the foot of the staircase towards the kitchen, and there had not been the faintest whimper from her, far less a bark. He was passing the dog basket when he had the most unnerving sensation of something being wrong there—something unusual, at least. He could not have said whether he had heard something or smelled something—he could certainly have seen nothing in the blackness; perhaps some extra sense warned him.

"Floss?" he whispered, and there was the usual little scrabble and snuffle. He held out his fingers low down for Floss to lick. As she did not do so at once, he moved them towards her, met some obstruction—

"Don't poke your fingers in my eye!" a voice said, very low-toned and cross. Charlie's first, confused thought was that Floss had spoken: the voice was familiar—but then a voice from Floss should *not* be familiar; it should be strangely new to him—

He took an uncertain little step towards the voice, tripped over the obstruction, which was quite wrong in shape and size to be Floss, and sat down. Two things now happened. Floss, apparently having climbed over the obstruction, reached his lap and began to lick his face. At the same time a human hand fumbled over his face, among the slappings of Floss's tongue, and settled over his mouth. "Don't make a row! Keep quiet!" said the same voice. Charlie's mind cleared; he knew, although without understanding, that he was sitting on the floor in the dark with Floss on his knee and Margaret beside him.

Her hand came off his mouth.

"What are you doing here anyway, Charlie?"

"I like that! What about you? There was a fly in my ear."

"Go on!"

"There was."

"Why does that make you come downstairs?"

"I wanted a drink of water."

"There's water in the bathroom."

"Well, I'm a bit hungry."

"If Mum catches you…."

"Look here," Charlie said, "you tell me what you're doing down here."

Margaret sighed. "Just sitting with Floss."

"You can't come down and just sit with Floss in the middle of the night."

"Yes, I can. I keep her company. Only at weekends, of course. No one seemed to realize what it was like for her when those puppies went. She just couldn't get to sleep for loneliness."

"But the last puppy went weeks ago. You haven't been keeping Floss company every Saturday night since then."

"Why not?"

Charlie gave up. "I'm going to get my food and drink," he said. He went into the kitchen, followed by Margaret, followed by Floss.

They all had a quick drink of water. Then Charlie and Margaret looked into the larder: the remains of a roast; a very large quantity of mashed potato; most of a loaf; eggs; butter; cheese…

"I suppose it'll have to be just bread and butter and a bit of cheese," said Charlie. "Else Mum might notice."

"Something hot," said Margaret. "I'm cold from sitting in the hall comforting Floss. I need hot cocoa, I think." She poured some milk into a saucepan and put it on the hot plate. Then she began a search for the cocoa. Charlie, standing by the cooker, was already absorbed in the making of a rough cheese sandwich.

The milk in the pan began to steam. Given time, it rose in the saucepan, peered over the top, and boiled over on to the hot plate, where it sizzled loudly. Margaret rushed back and pulled the saucepan to one side. "Well, really, Charlie! Now there's that awful smell! It'll still be here in the morning, too."

"Set the fan going," Charlie suggested.

The fan drew the smell from the cooker up and away through a pipe to the outside. It also made a loud roaring noise. Not loud enough to reach their parents, who slept on the other side of the house—that was all that Charlie and Margaret thought of.

Alison's bedroom, however, was immediately above the kitchen. Charlie was eating his bread and cheese, Margaret was drinking her cocoa, when the kitchen door opened and there stood Alison. Only Floss was pleased to see her.

"Well!" she said.

Charlie muttered something about a fly in his ear, but Margaret said nothing. Alison had caught them red-handed. She would call Mum downstairs, that was obvious. There would be an awful row.

Alison stood there. She liked commanding a situation.

Then, instead of taking a step backwards to call up the stairs to Mum, she took a step forward into the kitchen. "What are you having, anyway?" she asked. She glanced with scorn at Charlie's poor piece of bread and cheese and at Margaret's cocoa. She moved over to the larder, flung open the door, and looked searchingly inside. In such a way must Napoleon have viewed a battlefield before the victory.

Her gaze fell upon the bowl of mashed potato. "I shall make potato cakes," said Alison.

They watched while she brought the mashed potato to the kitchen table. She switched on the oven, fetched her other ingredients, and began mixing.

"Mum'll notice if you take much of that potato," said Margaret.

But Alison thought big. "She may notice if some potato is missing," she agreed. "But if there's none at all, and if the bowl it was in is washed and dried and stacked away with the others, then she's going to think she must have made a mistake. There just can never have been any mashed potato."

Alison rolled out her mixture and cut it into cakes; then she set the cakes on a baking tin and put it in the oven.

Now she did the washing up. Throughout the time they were in the kitchen, Alison washed up and put away as she went along. She wanted no one's help. She was very methodical, and she did everything herself to be sure that nothing was left undone. In the morning there must be no trace left of the cooking in the middle of the night.

"And now," said Alison, "I think we should fetch Wilson."

The other two were aghast at the idea; but Alison was firm in her reasons. "It's better if we're all in this together, Wilson as well. Then, if the worst comes to the worst, it won't be just us three caught out, with Wilson hanging on to Mum's apron strings, smiling innocence. We'll all be for it together; and Mum'll be softer with us if we've got Wilson."

They saw that, at once. But Margaret still objected. "Wilson will tell. He just always tells everything. He can't help it."

Alison said, "He always tells everything. Right. We'll give him something *to* tell, and then see if Mum believes him. We'll do an entertainment for him. Get an umbrella from the hall and Wilson's sou'wester and a blanket or a rug or something. Go on."

They would not obey Alison's orders until they had heard her plan; then they did. They fetched the umbrella and the hat, and lastly they fetched Wilson, still sound asleep, slung between the two of them in his eiderdown. They propped him in a chair at the kitchen table, where he still slept.

By now the potato cakes were done. Alison took them out of the oven and set them on the table before Wilson. She buttered them, handing them in turn to Charlie and Margaret and helping herself. One was set aside to cool for Floss.

The smell of fresh-cooked, buttery potato cake woke Wilson, as was to be expected. First his nose sipped the air; then his eyes opened; his gaze settled on the potato cakes.

"Like one?" Alison asked.

Wilson opened his mouth wide, and Alison put a potato cake inside, whole.

"They're paradise cakes," Alison said.

"Potato cakes?" said Wilson, recognizing the taste.

"No, paradise cakes, Wilson," and then, stepping aside, she gave him a clear view of Charlie's and Margaret's entertainment, with the umbrella and the sou'wester hat and his eiderdown. "Look, Wilson, look."

Wilson watched with wide-open eyes, and into his wide-open mouth Alison put, one by one, the potato cakes that were his share.

But, as they had foreseen, Wilson did not stay awake for very long. When there were no more potato cakes, he yawned, drowsed, and suddenly was deeply asleep. Charlie and Margaret put him back into his eiderdown and took him upstairs to bed again. They came down to return the umbrella and the sou'wester to their proper places, and to see Floss back into her basket. Alison, last out of the kitchen, made sure that everything was in its place.

The next morning Mum was down first. On Sunday she always cooked a proper breakfast for anyone there in time. Dad was always there in time; but this morning Mum was still looking for a bowl of mashed potato when he appeared.

"I can't think where it's gone," she said. "I can't think."

"I'll have the bacon and eggs without the potato," said Dad; and he did. While he ate, Mum went back to searching.

Wilson came down, and was sent upstairs again to put on a dressing gown. On his return he said that Charlie was still asleep and there was no sound from the girls' rooms either. He said he thought they were tired out. He went on talking while he ate his breakfast. Dad was reading the paper and Mum had gone back to poking about in the larder for the bowl of mashed potato, but Wilson liked talking even if no one would listen. When Mum came out of the larder for a moment, still without her potato, Wilson was saying: "...and Charlie sat in an umbrella boat on an eiderdown sea, and Margaret pretended to be a sea serpent, and Alison gave us paradise cakes to eat. Floss had one too, but it was too hot for her. What are paradise cakes? Dad, what's a paradise cake?"

"Don't know," said Dad, reading.

"Mum, what's a paradise cake?"

"Oh, Wilson, don't bother so when I'm looking for something.... When did you eat this cake, anyway?"

"I told you. Charlie sat in his umbrella boat on an eiderdown sea and Margaret was a sea serpent and Alison—"

"Wilson," said his mother, "you've been dreaming."

"No, really—really!" Wilson cried.

But his mother paid no further attention. "I give up," she said. "That mashed potato; it must have been last weekend…." She went out of the kitchen to call the others. "Charlie! Margaret! Alison!"

Wilson, in the kitchen, said to his father, "I wasn't dreaming. And Charlie said there was a fly in his ear."

Dad had been quarter-listening; now he put down his paper. "What?"

"Charlie had a fly in his ear."

Dad stared at Wilson. "And what did you say that Alison fed you with?"

"Paradise cakes. She'd just made them, I think, in the middle of the night."

"What were they like?"

"Lovely. Hot, with butter. Lovely."

"But were they—well, could they have had any mashed potato in them, for instance?"

In the hall Mum was finishing her calling. "Charlie! Margaret! Alison! I warn you now!"

"I don't know about that," Wilson said. "They were paradise cakes. They tasted a bit like the potato cakes Mum makes, but Alison said they weren't. She specially said they were paradise cakes."

Dad nodded. "You've finished your breakfast. Go up and get dressed, and you can take this"—he took a coin from his pocket— "straight off to the sweetshop. Go on."

Mum met Wilson at the kitchen door. "Where's he off too in such a hurry?"

"I gave him something to buy sweets with," said Dad. "I wanted a quiet breakfast. He talks too much."

Extending Comprehension

Story Questions

1. After Charlie has his battle with the fly and thinks the fly is dead, where does the fly reappear?
2. Which family members does Charlie wake up or try to wake up?
3. Why does Charlie decide to go to the kitchen?
4. What happens when Charlie holds out his fingers for his dog, Floss, to lick?
5. What does Charlie discover about Margaret and Floss?
6. Why do Charlie and Margaret have to turn on the fan?
7. What changes Alison's mind about tattling on her brother and sister?
8. How does Alison trick her mother into thinking there isn't any mashed potato missing?
9. Why does Alison think Wilson should be brought to the kitchen?
10. What is Alison's plan for making sure Wilson can't get the rest of the children in trouble with their parents?
11. What does Wilson describe the next morning?
12. What are Wilson's parents' reactions to his explanations?

Discussion Topics

1. There are several hilarious scenes in this story; for example, when the fly and Charlie battle, when Charlie discovers Floss and Margaret, and when the older children entertain and feed Wilson in the middle of the night. Pick your favorite scene and expand it, writing dialogue as needed. Be sure to use the kind of words that each character would say. Then read your scene to the rest of the class.

2. The way the family members in this story interact with each other seems fairly typical. Think about the interactions between the children and the interactions between the children and their parents. In what ways do the characters remind you of your family? In what ways is your family different from the family in the story?

Writing Ideas

1. The author does an excellent job of helping her readers create funny mental pictures. Write about something funny that happened to you or that you observed. Describe the situation well enough so your readers get a clear mental picture of the scene. You may want to write some dialogue to accompany your description. See if you can make people laugh out loud when they read what you wrote.

2. You can use your imagination to answer some questions about the people in the story. For example, do you think Charlie's mom ever figures out whether or not there had been a mashed potato? How could she find out? Do you think his dad already knows the answer? Write your answers to these questions. Write out any other questions you may have.

3. Write a description of Alison that includes evidence from the story supporting the statement "Alison is a smart and clever girl."

THE SHRINKING OF TREEHORN

by Florence Parry Heide · Illustrated by Edward Gorey

New Vocabulary Words

1. Treehorn
2. shrinking
3. stretching

4. rummage around
5. whistles that make a very high sound

6. shirk
7. water bubbler

Definitions

1. **Treehorn** is the unusual first name of the main character in "The Shrinking of Treehorn."
2. **Shrinking** is another way of saying *growing smaller.*
3. **Stretching** is another way of saying *growing bigger.*
4. When you **rummage around,** you look through a lot of things to find what you are looking for.
5. Only dogs can hear **whistles that make a very high sound.** Dogs can hear higher-pitched sounds than people.
6. When you **shirk** your responsibilities, you put them off or avoid them. A person who avoids work can be called a shirker.
7. A **water bubbler** is a type of drinking fountain.

Story Background

"The Shrinking of Treehorn" is a humorous short story about a boy who keeps getting smaller. The people in the story don't listen to what other people are saying, and they don't see obvious problems.

Characters who shrink and then grow back to their normal size appear in several well-known stories. Perhaps the most famous of these stories is *Alice's Adventures in Wonderland,* by Lewis Carroll. In the story, Alice shrinks to the size of a mouse, opens a tiny door, and enters a place called Wonderland, where she has many adventures. In one of those adventures, she suddenly grows back to her normal size.

Unlike Alice, Treehorn doesn't enter Wonderland when he shrinks. Instead, he keeps living in the same old house and going to the same old school. The only thing that changes is his size.

THE SHRINKING OF TREEHORN

by Florence Parry Heide · *illustrated by Edward Gorey*

Focus Questions

- For how many days does Treehorn shrink?
- How do Treehorn's parents, friends, teachers, principal, and the other people he meets respond to his problem?

Something very strange was happening to Treehorn.

The first thing he noticed was that he couldn't reach the shelf in his closet that he had always been able to reach before, the one where he hid his candy bars and bubble gum.

Then he noticed that his clothes were getting too big.

"My trousers are all stretching or something," said Treehorn to his mother. "I'm tripping on them all the time."

"That's too bad, dear," said his mother, looking into the oven. "I do hope this cake isn't going to fall," she said.

"And my sleeves come down way below my hands," said Treehorn. "So my shirts must be stretching, too."

"Think of that," said Treehorn's mother. "I just don't know why this cake isn't rising the way it should. Mrs. Abernale's cakes are *always* nice. They *always* rise."

Treehorn started out of the kitchen. He tripped on his trousers, which indeed did seem to be getting longer and longer.

At dinner that night Treehorn's father said, "Do sit up, Treehorn. I can hardly see your head."

"I *am* sitting up," said Treehorn. "This is as far up as I come. I think I must be shrinking or something."

"I'm sorry my cake didn't turn out very well," said Treehorn's mother.

"It's very nice, dear," said Treehorn's father politely.

By this time Treehorn could hardly see over the top of the table.

"Sit up, dear," said Treehorn's mother.

"I *am* sitting up," said Treehorn. "It's just that I'm shrinking."

"What, dear?" asked his mother.

"I'm shrinking. Getting smaller," said Treehorn.

"If you want to pretend you're shrinking, that's all right," said Treehorn's mother, "as long as you don't do it at the table."

"But I *am* shrinking," said Treehorn.

"Don't argue with your mother, Treehorn," said Treehorn's father.

"He does look a little smaller," said Treehorn's mother, looking at Treehorn. "Maybe he *is* shrinking."

"Nobody shrinks," said Treehorn's father.

"Well, I'm shrinking," said Treehorn. "Look at me."

Treehorn's father looked at Treehorn.

"Why, you're shrinking," said Treehorn's father. "Look, Emily, Treehorn is shrinking. He's much smaller than he used to be."

"Oh, dear," said Treehorn's mother. "First it was the cake, and now it's this. Everything happens at once."

"I *thought* I was shrinking," said Treehorn, and he went into the den to turn on the television set.

Treehorn liked to watch television. Now he lay on his stomach in front of the television set and watched one of his favorite programs. He had fifty-six favorite programs.

During the commercials, Treehorn always listened to his mother and father talking together, unless they were having a boring conversation. If they were having a boring conversation, he listened to the commercials.

Now he listened to his mother and father.

"He really is getting smaller," said Treehorn's mother. "What will we do? What will people say?"

"Why, they'll say he's getting smaller," said Treehorn's father. He thought for a moment. "I wonder if he's doing it on purpose. Just to be different."

"Why would he want to be different?" asked Treehorn's mother.

Treehorn started listening to the commercial.

The next morning Treehorn was still smaller. His regular clothes were much too big to wear. He rummaged around in his closet until he found some of his last year's clothes. They were much too big, too, but he put them on and rolled up the pants and rolled up the sleeves and went down to breakfast.

Treehorn liked cereal for breakfast. But mostly he liked cereal boxes. He always read every single thing on the cereal box while he was eating breakfast. And he always sent in for the things the cereal box said he could send for.

In a box in his closet Treehorn saved all of the things he had sent in for from cereal box tops. He had puzzles and special rings and flashlights and pictures of all of the presidents and pictures of all of the baseball players and he had pictures of scenes suitable for framing, which he had never framed because he didn't like them very much, and he had all kinds of games and pens and models.

Today on the cereal box was a very special offer of a very special whistle that only dogs could hear. Treehorn did not have a dog, but he thought it would be nice to have a whistle that dogs could hear, even if *he* couldn't hear it. Even if *dogs* couldn't hear it, it would be nice to have a whistle, just to have it.

He decided to eat all of the cereal in the box so he could send in this morning for the whistle. His mother never let him send in for anything until he had eaten all of the cereal in the box.

Treehorn filled in all of the blank spaces for his name and address and then he went to get his money out of the piggy bank on the kitchen counter, but he couldn't reach it.

"I certainly *am* getting smaller," thought Treehorn. He climbed up on a chair and got the piggy bank and shook out a dime.

His mother was cleaning the refrigerator. "You know how I hate to have you climb up on the chairs, dear," she said. She went into the living room to dust.

Treehorn put the piggy bank in the bottom kitchen drawer.

"That way I can get it no matter *how* little I get," he thought.

He found an envelope and put a stamp on it and put the dime and the box top in so he could mail the letter on the way to school. The mailbox was right next to the bus stop.

It was hard to walk to the bus stop because his shoes kept slipping off, but he got there in plenty of time, shuffling. He couldn't reach the mailbox slot to put the letter in, so he handed the letter to one of his friends, Moshie, and asked him to put it in. Moshie put it in. "How come you can't mail it yourself, stupid?" asked Moshie.

"Because I'm shrinking," explained Treehorn. "I'm shrinking and I'm too little to reach the mailbox."

"That's a stupid thing to do," said Moshie. "You're *always* doing stupid things, but that's the *stupidest*."

When Treehorn tried to get on the school bus, everyone was pushing and shoving. The bus driver said, "All the way back in the bus, step all the way back." Then he saw Treehorn trying to climb onto the bus.

"Let that little kid on," said the bus driver.

Treehorn was helped onto the bus. The bus driver said, "You can stay right up here next to me if you want to, because you're so little."

"It's me, Treehorn," said Treehorn to his friend the bus driver.

The bus driver looked down at Treehorn. "You do look like Treehorn, at that," he said. "Only smaller. Treehorn isn't that little."

"I am Treehorn. I'm just getting smaller," said Treehorn.

"Nobody gets smaller," said the bus driver. "You must be Treehorn's kid brother. What's your name?"

"Treehorn," said Treehorn.

"First time I ever heard of a family naming two boys the same name," said the bus driver. "Guess they couldn't think of any other name, once they thought of Treehorn."

Treehorn said nothing.

When he went into class, his teacher said, "Nursery school is down at the end of the hall, honey."

"I'm Treehorn," said Treehorn.

"If you're Treehorn, why are you so small?" asked the teacher.

"Because I'm shrinking," said Treehorn. "I'm getting smaller."

"Well, I'll let it go for today," said his teacher. "But see that it's taken care of before tomorrow. We don't shrink in this class."

After recess, Treehorn was thirsty, so he went down the hall to the water bubbler. He couldn't reach it, and he tried to jump up high enough. He still couldn't get a drink, but he kept jumping up and down, trying.

His teacher walked by. "Why, Treehorn," she said. "That isn't like you, jumping up and down in the hall. Just because you're shrinking, it does not mean you have special privileges. What if all the children in the *school* started jumping up and down in the halls? I'm afraid you'll have to go to the Principal's office, Treehorn."

So Treehorn went to the Principal's office.

"I'm supposed to see the Principal," said Treehorn to the lady in the Principal's outer office.

"It's a very busy day," said the lady. "Please check here on this form the reason you have to see him. That will save time. Be sure to put your name down, too. That will save time. And write clearly. That will save time."

Treehorn looked at the form:

CHECK REASON YOU HAVE TO SEE PRINCIPAL (that will save time)
☐ 1. Talking in class
☐ 2. Chewing gum in class
☐ 3. Talking back to teacher
☐ 4. Unexcused absence
☐ 5. Unexcused illness
☐ 6. Unexcused behavior

P.T.O.

There were many things to check, but Treehorn couldn't find one that said "Being Too Small to Reach the Water Bubbler." He finally wrote in "SHRINKING."

When the lady said he could see the Principal, Treehorn went into the Principal's office with his form.

The Principal looked at the form, and then he looked at Treehorn. Then he looked at the form again.

"I can't read this," said the Principal. "It looks like SHIRKING. You're not SHIRKING, are you, Treehorn? We can't have any shirkers here, you know. We're a team, and we all have to do our very best."

"It says SHRINKING," said Treehorn. "I'm shrinking."

"Shrinking, eh?" said the Principal. "Well, now, I'm very sorry to hear that, Treehorn. You were right to come to me. That's what I'm here for. To guide. Not to punish, but to guide. To guide all the members of my team. To solve all their problems."

"But I don't have any problems," said Treehorn. "I'm just shrinking."

"Well, I want you to know I'm right here when you need me, Treehorn," said the Principal, "and I'm glad I was here to help you. A team is only as good as its coach, eh?"

The Principal stood up. "Goodbye, Treehorn. If you have any more problems, come straight to me, and I'll help you again. A problem isn't a problem once it's solved, right?"

By the end of the day Treehorn was still smaller.

At the dinner table that night he sat on several cushions so he could be high enough to see over the top of the table.

"He's still shrinking," sniffed Treehorn's mother. "Heaven knows I've *tried* to be a good mother."

"Maybe we should call a doctor," said Treehorn's father.

"I did," said Treehorn's mother. "I called every doctor in the Yellow Pages. But no one knew anything about shrinking problems."

She sniffed again. "Maybe he'll just keep getting smaller and smaller until he disappears."

"No one disappears," said Treehorn's father positively.

"That's right, they don't," said Treehorn's mother more cheerfully. "But no one shrinks, either," she said after a moment. "Finish your carrots, Treehorn."

The next morning Treehorn was so small he had to jump out of bed. On the floor under the bed was a game he'd pushed under there and forgotten about. He walked under the bed to look at it.

It was one of the games he had sent in for from a cereal box. He had started playing it a couple of days ago, but he hadn't had a chance to finish it because his mother had called him to come right downstairs that minute and have his breakfast or he'd be late for school.

Treehorn looked at the cover of the box:

THE BIG GAME FOR KIDS TO GROW ON

IT'S TREMENDOUS! IT'S DIFFERENT!
IT'S FUN! IT'S EASY! IT'S COLOSSAL!
PLAY IT WITH FRIENDS!
PLAY IT ALONE!

Complete with Spinner, Board, Pieces, and–!
COMPLETE INSTRUCTIONS!

The game was called THE *BIG* GAME FOR KIDS TO GROW ON.

Treehorn sat under the bed to finish playing the game.

He always liked to finish things, even if they were boring. Even if he was watching a boring program on TV, he always watched it right to the end. Games were the same way. He'd finish this one now. Where had he left off? He remembered he'd just had to move his piece back seven spaces on the board when his mother had called him.

He was so small now that the only way he could move the spinner was by kicking it, so he kicked it. It stopped at number 4. That meant he could move his piece ahead four spaces on the board.

The only way he could move the piece forward now was by carrying it, so he carried it. It was pretty heavy. He walked along the board to the fourth space. It said CONGRATULATIONS, AND UP YOU GO: ADVANCE THIRTEEN SPACES.

Treehorn started to carry his piece forward the thirteen spaces, but the piece seemed to be getting smaller. Or else *he* was getting *bigger*. That was it, he *was* getting bigger, because the bottom of the bed was getting close to his head. He pulled the game out from under the bed to finish playing it.

He kept moving the piece forward, but he didn't have to carry it any longer. In fact, he seemed to be getting bigger and bigger with each space he landed in.

"Well, I don't want to get *too* big," thought Treehorn. So he moved the piece ahead slowly from one space to the next, getting bigger with each space, until he was his own regular size again. Then he put the spinner and the pieces and the instructions and the board back in the box for THE *BIG* GAME FOR KIDS TO GROW ON and put it in his closet. If he ever wanted to get bigger or smaller he could play it again, even if it *was* a pretty boring game.

Treehorn went down for breakfast and started to read the new cereal box. It said you could send for a hundred balloons. His mother was cleaning the living room. She came into the kitchen to get a dust rag.

"Don't put your elbows on the table while you're eating, dear," she said.

"Look," said Treehorn. "I'm my own size now. My own regular size."

"That's nice, dear," said Treehorn's mother. "It's a very nice size, I'm sure, and if I were you I wouldn't shrink anymore. Be sure to tell your father when he comes home tonight. He'll be so pleased." She went back to the living room and started to dust and vacuum.

That night Treehorn was watching TV. As he reached over to change channels, he noticed that his hand was bright green. He looked in the mirror that was hanging over the television set. His face was green. His ears were green. His hair was green. He was green all over.

Treehorn sighed. "I don't think I'll tell anyone," he thought to himself. "If I don't say anything, they won't notice."

Treehorn's mother came in. "Do turn the volume down a little, dear," she said. "Your father and I are having the Smedleys over to play bridge. Do comb your hair before they come, won't you, dear," said his mother as she walked back to the kitchen.

Extending Comprehension

Story Questions

1. How does Treehorn discover that he is shrinking?
2. What interests Treehorn's mother more than Treehorn's problem?
3. What explanation does Treehorn's father give for why Treehorn is shrinking?
4. Describe four of the problems Treehorn has before he gets to school.
5. How does Treehorn solve those problems?
6. Why does Treenhorn's teacher send him to the principal's office?
7. What word does the principal have trouble reading? What word does he think it is?
8. What is the name of the game that Treehorn finds under his bed?
9. How does the game help Treehorn grow back to his normal size?
10. What happens to Treehorn at the very end of the story?

Discussion Topics

1. What the characters say in "The Shrinking of Treehorn" can be very funny when the words are read out loud. Divide the "The Shrinking of Treehorn" into three sections: the first day, the second day, and the third day. Determine which groups of 5 or 6 students will take each section. Decide which students will read what the different characters say in the story. Other students will read the sentences that provide the background for what the characters say. The first-day group will read the first-day part of the story out loud; the second-day group will read the second-day part of the story out loud; the third-day group will read the third-day part of the story out loud.

2. At the end of the story, Treehorn says to himself, "I don't think I'll tell anyone. If I don't say anything, they won't notice." Why do you think he says those things? During your discussion, try to answer the following questions:
   - What happens when Treehorn tells his parents about his problem?
   - What happens when Treehorn tells his friend, Moshie, about his problem?
   - What happens when Treehorn talks about his problem with the bus driver?
   - What happens when Treehorn talks to the principal?
   - Why do you think Treehorn says, "If I don't say anything, they won't notice"?
   - What do you think the author's purpose is in writing the story?

Writing Ideas

1. Suppose you wake up one morning and all of your clothes are too big for you. What will you say to the people you see? Write what you will say to explain your new size. Then think of some of the advantages and disadvantages of being small, and write about them.

2. Much of the action in the story "The Shrinking of Treehorn" is conveyed by dialogue. **Dialogue** is a conversation between two or more people. Treehorn has conversations with a lot of people. Pick a place in the story you especially like, and write some additional dialogue that could have taken place between Treehorn and another character. For example, you might write the dialogue that Treehorn and his teacher have after Treehorn comes back from the principal's office.

3. Think about a time when you felt that an adult didn't really listen to what you were saying. Tell about what you were trying to say, who you were saying it to, and how you felt. Think about why that adult might not have been listening to you. What reasons do you think that person had for not listening?

The Gallant Tailor

by The Brothers Grimm
Illustrated by Carolyn Bracken

New Vocabulary Words

1. tailor
2. cunning
3. unmercifully
4. feat

5. comrade
6. rascal
7. sprig
8. vault

9. den
10. elbow room
11. courtier
12. waistcoat
13. britches

Definitions

1. A **tailor** is a person who makes or repairs clothes.
2. A **cunning** person is a crafty person.
3. If you hit something **unmercifully,** you hit that thing very, very hard. You have no mercy on it.
4. A **feat** is an important accomplishment.
5. Good friends are **comrades.**
6. A **rascal** is a playful person who may also be dishonest.
7. A tiny twig from a plant is a **sprig.**

8. When you **vault** something, you jump over it.
9. A **den** is a hiding place. Bears spend the winter in their dens.
10. **Elbow room** is an expression that means having lots of space.
11. A **courtier** is a man who serves in the court of a king or queen. Some kings and queens had many courtiers.
12. A **waistcoat** is a short, sleeveless vest.
13. **Britches** are trousers that end at the knee.

Story Background

"The Gallant Tailor" is a type of story called a folktale. Many folktales are old stories that people told aloud. Parents told these stories to their children, and when the children became parents themselves, they told the same stories to their own children. Some stories were passed on this way for hundreds of years without ever being written down.

In the early 1800s, two brothers from Germany named Jacob and Wilhelm Grimm began listening to folktales and writing them down. The folktales they collected were from Germany and other countries in Europe. Many of these folktales were hundreds of years old.

"The Gallant Tailor" is about a man who gains a great deal by outwitting other people and by exaggerating his accomplishments. Like many folktales, the story is told as a **sequence,** or chain of events. What happens in one event leads to what happens in the next event. After each event, the little tailor becomes more important. Also, as is true in some other folktales, this story is about a little person who is smarter and craftier than the more powerful and important people he meets.

The title of the story, "The Gallant Tailor," may also be an exaggeration. *Gallant* can mean noble and extremely polite. When you finish reading about the many adventures of the little tailor, you decide if he is a gallant man. Think of some other words you might use to describe him.

Focus Questions

- What are the different events on the tailor's journey?
- How does the tailor become more important after each event in the story?

The Gallant Tailor

by The Brothers Grimm
Illustrated by Carolyn Bracken

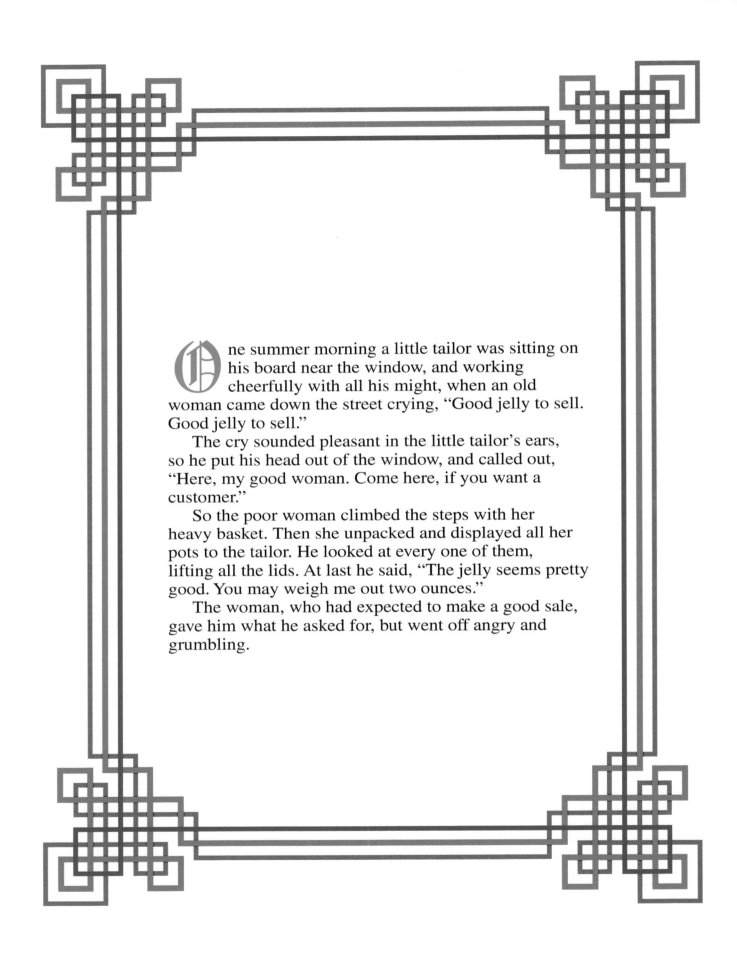

One summer morning a little tailor was sitting on his board near the window, and working cheerfully with all his might, when an old woman came down the street crying, "Good jelly to sell. Good jelly to sell."

The cry sounded pleasant in the little tailor's ears, so he put his head out of the window, and called out, "Here, my good woman. Come here, if you want a customer."

So the poor woman climbed the steps with her heavy basket. Then she unpacked and displayed all her pots to the tailor. He looked at every one of them, lifting all the lids. At last he said, "The jelly seems pretty good. You may weigh me out two ounces."

The woman, who had expected to make a good sale, gave him what he asked for, but went off angry and grumbling.

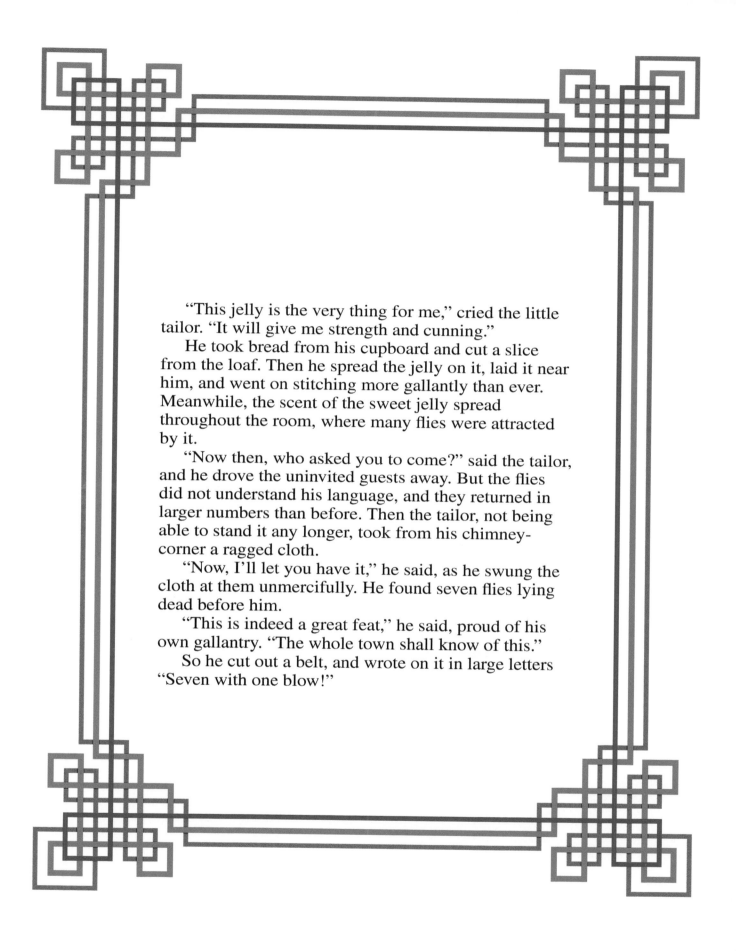

"This jelly is the very thing for me," cried the little tailor. "It will give me strength and cunning."

He took bread from his cupboard and cut a slice from the loaf. Then he spread the jelly on it, laid it near him, and went on stitching more gallantly than ever. Meanwhile, the scent of the sweet jelly spread throughout the room, where many flies were attracted by it.

"Now then, who asked you to come?" said the tailor, and he drove the uninvited guests away. But the flies did not understand his language, and they returned in larger numbers than before. Then the tailor, not being able to stand it any longer, took from his chimney-corner a ragged cloth.

"Now, I'll let you have it," he said, as he swung the cloth at them unmercifully. He found seven flies lying dead before him.

"This is indeed a great feat," he said, proud of his own gallantry. "The whole town shall know of this."

So he cut out a belt, and wrote on it in large letters "Seven with one blow!"

"The town, did I say?" said the little tailor. "The whole world shall know it!" And his heart quivered with joy, like a lamb's tail.

The tailor fastened the belt around him, and he began to think of going out into the world, for his workshop seemed too small for the worship he would receive. So he looked about in all the house for something that would be useful to take with him. He found nothing but an old cheese, which he put in his pocket.

Outside the door, he noticed that a bird was caught in the bushes, so he took that bird and put it in his pocket with the cheese. Then he set out gallantly on his way, and as he was light and active he felt no fatigue. The path led over a mountain, and when he reached the topmost peak he saw a terrible giant sitting there, looking around.

The tailor went bravely up to him, called out to him and said, "Comrade, good day. There you sit looking over the wide world. I am on the way to seek my fortune. Would you like to go with me?"

The giant looked at the tailor with contempt and said, "You little rascal. You miserable fellow."

"That may be," answered the little tailor, who opened his coat and showed the giant his belt. "You can read there whether I am a man or not!"

The giant read "Seven with one blow!" Thinking the belt meant seven men that the tailor had killed, he felt at once more respect for the little fellow. But to test him, he took up a stone and squeezed it so hard that water came out of it.

"Now you can do the same thing," said the giant. "If you have the strength for it."

"That's not much," said the little tailor, "I call that play." And he put his hand in his pocket and took out the cheese and squeezed it, so that the moisture ran out of it.

"Well," said the tailor, "what do you think of that?"

The giant did not know what to say, for he could not have believed it of the little man. Then the giant took up a stone and threw it so high that it was nearly out of sight.

"Now, little fellow, suppose you do that."

"Well thrown," said the tailor. "But the stone fell back to earth again. I will throw you one that will never come back." So he felt in his pocket, took out the bird and threw it into the air. And the bird took wing, flew off, and returned no more.

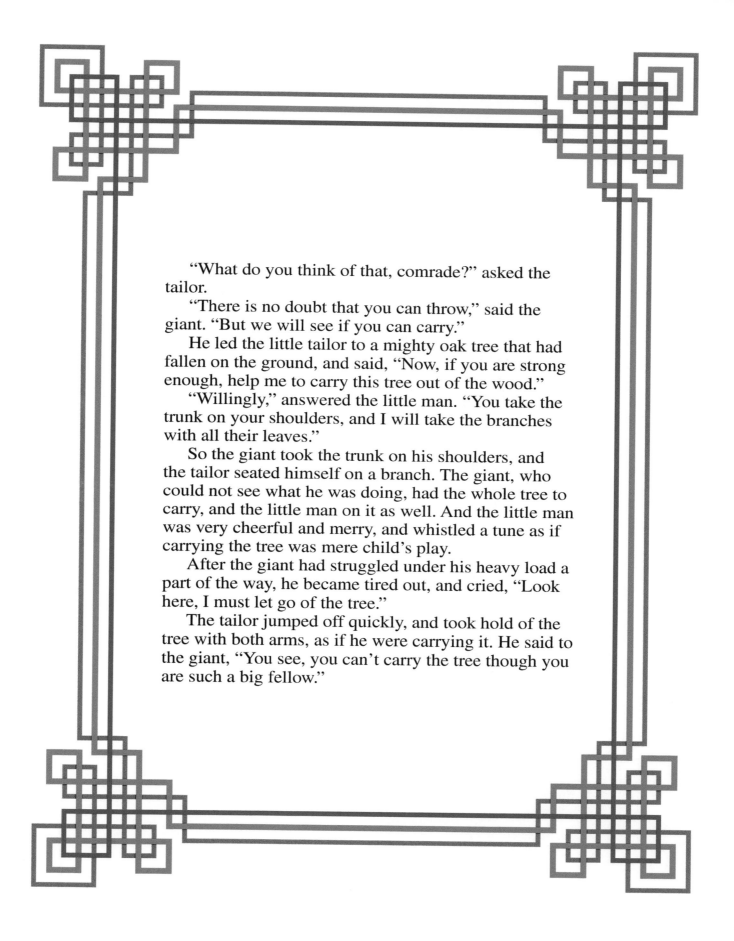

"What do you think of that, comrade?" asked the tailor.

"There is no doubt that you can throw," said the giant. "But we will see if you can carry."

He led the little tailor to a mighty oak tree that had fallen on the ground, and said, "Now, if you are strong enough, help me to carry this tree out of the wood."

"Willingly," answered the little man. "You take the trunk on your shoulders, and I will take the branches with all their leaves."

So the giant took the trunk on his shoulders, and the tailor seated himself on a branch. The giant, who could not see what he was doing, had the whole tree to carry, and the little man on it as well. And the little man was very cheerful and merry, and whistled a tune as if carrying the tree was mere child's play.

After the giant had struggled under his heavy load a part of the way, he became tired out, and cried, "Look here, I must let go of the tree."

The tailor jumped off quickly, and took hold of the tree with both arms, as if he were carrying it. He said to the giant, "You see, you can't carry the tree though you are such a big fellow."

They went on together a little farther, and presently they came to a cherry tree, and the giant took hold of the topmost branches, where the ripest fruit hung. Pulling them downward, he gave them to the tailor to hold, bidding him eat. But the little tailor was much too weak to hold the tree. As the giant let go, the tree sprang back, and the tailor flew up into the air. And when he dropped down again without any damage, the giant said to him, "How is this? Haven't you strength enough to hold such a weak sprig as that?"

"It is not strength that is lacking," answered the little tailor. "Remember I am a man who has slain seven with one blow. I just jumped over the tree because the hunters are shooting down there in the bushes. You jump it too, if you can."

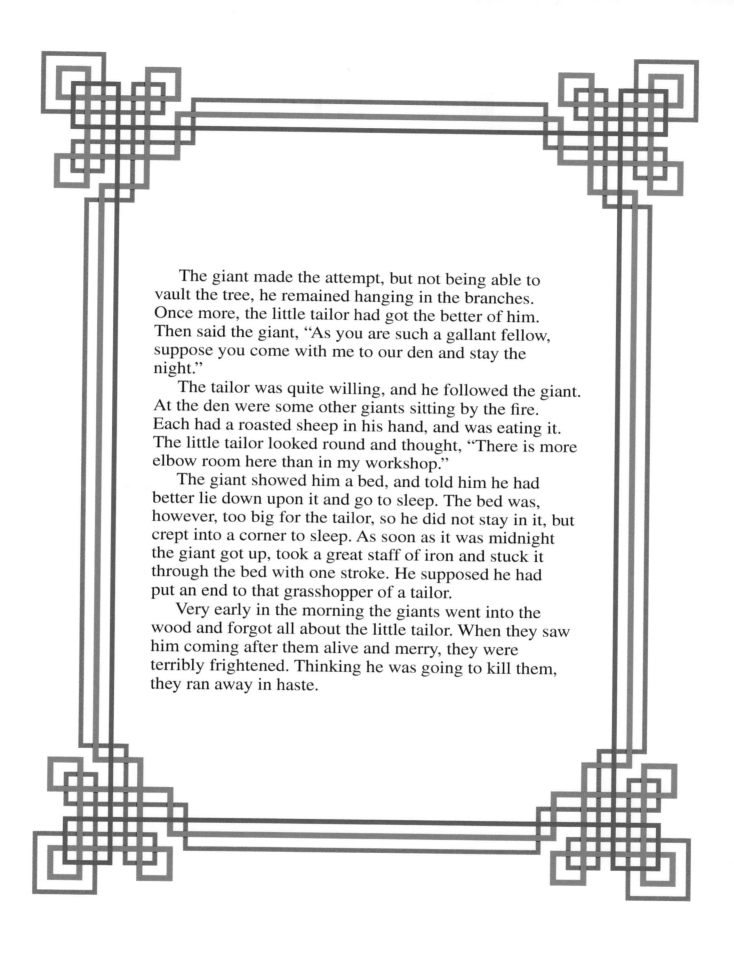

The giant made the attempt, but not being able to vault the tree, he remained hanging in the branches. Once more, the little tailor had got the better of him. Then said the giant, "As you are such a gallant fellow, suppose you come with me to our den and stay the night."

The tailor was quite willing, and he followed the giant. At the den were some other giants sitting by the fire. Each had a roasted sheep in his hand, and was eating it. The little tailor looked round and thought, "There is more elbow room here than in my workshop."

The giant showed him a bed, and told him he had better lie down upon it and go to sleep. The bed was, however, too big for the tailor, so he did not stay in it, but crept into a corner to sleep. As soon as it was midnight the giant got up, took a great staff of iron and stuck it through the bed with one stroke. He supposed he had put an end to that grasshopper of a tailor.

Very early in the morning the giants went into the wood and forgot all about the little tailor. When they saw him coming after them alive and merry, they were terribly frightened. Thinking he was going to kill them, they ran away in haste.

So the little tailor marched on, always following his nose. And after he had gone a great way he entered the courtyard of a king's palace. There he felt so overpowered with fatigue that he lay down and fell asleep. In the meanwhile various people came by. They looked at him curiously and read on his belt, "Seven with one blow."

"Oh," said they, "why should this great lord come here in peace? What a mighty champion he must be!"

Then they went and told the king about him. They thought that if war should break out what a worthy and useful man he would be, and that he should not be allowed to leave. The king then sent one of his courtiers to the little tailor to beg him to serve in the king's army.

So the messenger stood and waited at the sleeper's side until his eyes began to open. Then he asked the tailor to join the king's army.

"That was the reason I came here," said the little tailor. "I am ready to serve the king."

So he was received into the army very honorably, and a special dwelling was set up for him. But the rest of the soldiers resented the little tailor, and they wished that he was a thousand miles away.

"What shall be done about it?" they said among themselves. "If we pick a quarrel and fight with him then seven of us will fall with each blow. That will be no good."

So they all went together to the king to ask to be released from the army. "We never intended," said they, "to serve with a man who kills seven with a blow." The king felt sorry to lose all his faithful servants because of one man, and he wished that he had never seen him. But he did not dare to dismiss the little tailor for fear he would kill all the king's people and place himself upon the throne. He thought a long while about it, and at last made up his mind what to do.

The king sent for the little tailor and told him that he had a proposal. He told the tailor that in a forest lived two giants, who did great damage by robbery, murder and fire. No man dared go near them. If the tailor could slay both these giants, the king would give him his only daughter in marriage, and half his kingdom as well. What's more, a hundred horsemen would go with him to give him assistance.

"That would be something for a man like me," thought the little tailor. "A beautiful princess and half a kingdom are not to be had every day." So he said to the king, "Oh yes, I can easily take care of the giants. He who can kill seven with one blow has no need to be afraid of two."

So the little tailor set out, and the hundred horsemen followed him. When he came to the border of the forest he said to his escort, "Stay here while I go to attack the giants."

Then he sprang into the wood, and looked about him right and left. After a while he caught sight of the two giants. They were lying down under a tree asleep, and snoring so that all the branches shook. The little tailor filled both his pockets with stones and climbed up into the tree. He made his way to an overhanging bough, so that he could seat himself just above the sleepers. From there, he let one stone after another fall on the chest of one of the giants.

For a long time the giant was unaware of the stones, but at last he woke up and pushed his comrade, and said, "What are you hitting me for?"

"You are dreaming," said the other. "I am not touching you." And they went back to sleep. Then the tailor let a stone fall on the other giant.

He cried, "What are you throwing at me?"

"I am not throwing anything at you," answered the first.

They argued about it for a while, but because they were tired, they gave it up at last, and their eyes closed once more. Then the little tailor began his game again. He picked out a heavier stone and threw it down with force upon the first giant's chest.

"This is too much!" cried that giant, and he sprang up like a madman and struck his companion such a blow that the tree shook above them. The other struck back, and they fought with such fury that they tore up trees by their roots to use for weapons against each other. At last both of them lay dead upon the ground. And now the little tailor climbed down.

"Another piece of luck," said he. "The tree I was sitting in did not get torn up too, or else I would have had to jump like a squirrel from one tree to another."

Then he drew his sword and gave each of the giants a few hacks in the breast. He went back to the horsemen and said, "The deed is done. I have made an end of both of them. In the struggle they rooted up trees to defend themselves, but it was of no use. They had to deal with a man who can kill seven with one blow."

"Are you not wounded?" asked the horsemen.

"Nothing of the sort," answered the tailor. "I don't have one hair out of place."

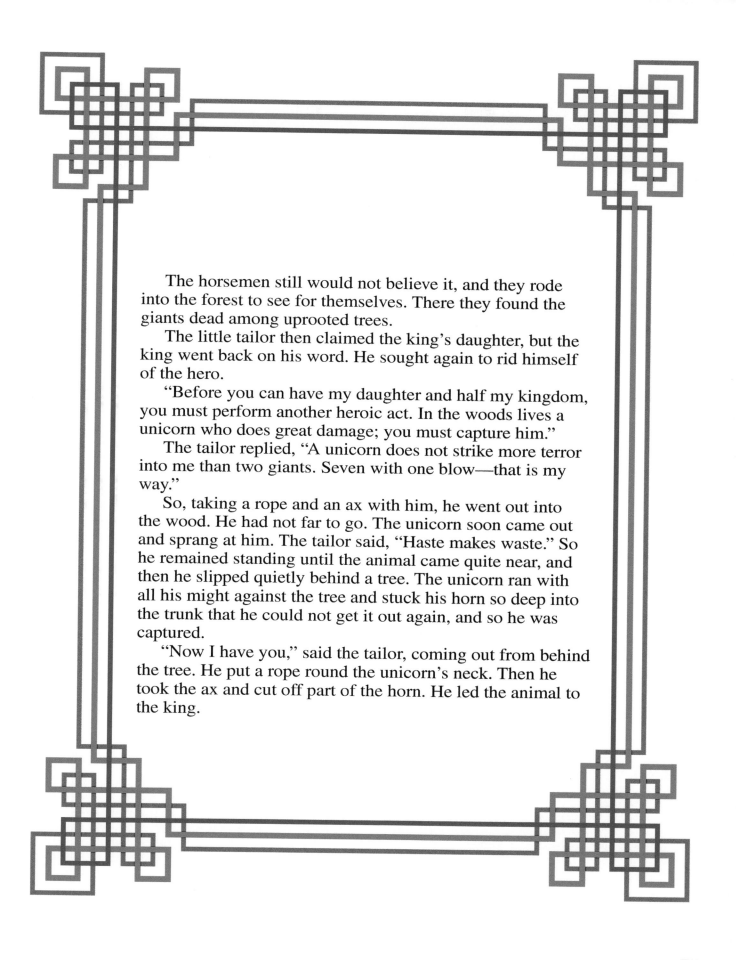

The horsemen still would not believe it, and they rode into the forest to see for themselves. There they found the giants dead among uprooted trees.

The little tailor then claimed the king's daughter, but the king went back on his word. He sought again to rid himself of the hero.

"Before you can have my daughter and half my kingdom, you must perform another heroic act. In the woods lives a unicorn who does great damage; you must capture him."

The tailor replied, "A unicorn does not strike more terror into me than two giants. Seven with one blow—that is my way."

So, taking a rope and an ax with him, he went out into the wood. He had not far to go. The unicorn soon came out and sprang at him. The tailor said, "Haste makes waste." So he remained standing until the animal came quite near, and then he slipped quietly behind a tree. The unicorn ran with all his might against the tree and stuck his horn so deep into the trunk that he could not get it out again, and so he was captured.

"Now I have you," said the tailor, coming out from behind the tree. He put a rope round the unicorn's neck. Then he took the ax and cut off part of the horn. He led the animal to the king.

The king did not yet wish to give the tailor the promised reward, so he set him a third task to do. Before the wedding could take place the tailor was to catch a wild boar that had done a great deal of damage in the woods.

The huntsmen were to accompany him.

"All right," said the tailor, "this is child's play."

But he did not take the huntsmen into the woods. They were happy about that, for they had no desire to disturb the wild boar.

When the boar caught sight of the tailor he charged with foaming mouth and gleaming tusks. But the nimble hero rushed into a chapel and jumped quickly out of a window on the other side. The boar ran after him, and when he got inside, the tailor slammed the door shut after him. And there the boar was imprisoned. The creature was too big to jump out of the window.

Then the little tailor called the huntsmen that they might see the prisoner with their own eyes. He then returned to the king, who was obliged to fulfill his promise. The wedding was celebrated with great splendor but little joy. The tailor was made into a king.

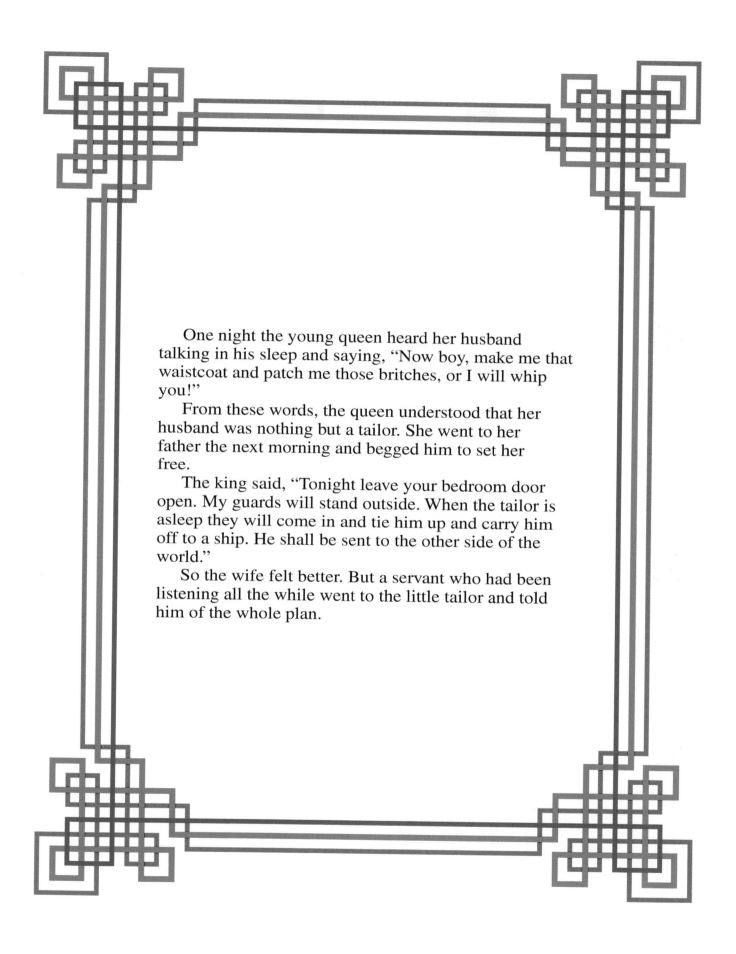

One night the young queen heard her husband talking in his sleep and saying, "Now boy, make me that waistcoat and patch me those britches, or I will whip you!"

From these words, the queen understood that her husband was nothing but a tailor. She went to her father the next morning and begged him to set her free.

The king said, "Tonight leave your bedroom door open. My guards will stand outside. When the tailor is asleep they will come in and tie him up and carry him off to a ship. He shall be sent to the other side of the world."

So the wife felt better. But a servant who had been listening all the while went to the little tailor and told him of the whole plan.

"I shall put a stop to all this," said the tailor.

At night he lay down as usual in bed. When his wife thought he was asleep, she got up, opened the door and lay down again. The little tailor, who only pretended to be asleep, began to murmur plainly.

"Now, boy, make me that waistcoat and patch me those britches, or I will whip you! I have slain seven with one blow, killed two giants, caught a unicorn and taken a wild boar. Why should I be afraid of those who are standing outside my room?"

And when the guards heard the tailor say this, a great fear seized them. They fled away like wild hares.

And so the little tailor remained a king for the rest of his life.

Extending Comprehension

Story Questions

1. How do the people the little tailor meets interpret the message on his belt?
2. Why does the giant call the tailor a "rascal and miserable fellow"?
3. How does the tailor use the cheese and the bird to impress the giant?
4. How does the tailor trick the giant into thinking he is helping the giant carry the tree?
5. When he is in the giant's den, what saves the tailor from the giant's attack?
6. Why do the people at the palace tell the king about the sleeping tailor?
7. Why do the king's soldiers resent the little tailor?
8. What does the king promise the little tailor if he would slay the two giants who lived in the forest?
9. How does the little tailor trick the two giants?
10. Why does the king want to get rid of the little tailor?
11. The little tailor has to do two more things before the king rewards him. What are they?
12. How does the young queen learn that her husband is "nothing but a tailor"?
13. What does the king say he would do?
14. How does the little tailor frighten the guards?

Discussion Topics

1. "The Gallant Tailor" is about a little man who resolves many problems, not because he is strong as he claims, but because he is clever and cunning. Discuss the events of the story and how the little tailor resolves each of the problems. During your discussion, try to answer the following questions:

   - How many times does the tailor find the message on his belt useful? Describe those situations.
   - How does he take advantage of each of the people he meets—the first giant, the two giants, the soldiers, and the king?
   - Do you think the little tailor is gallant?

2. The little tailor is full of self-confidence. Discuss some of the times he lets the people he meets know how confident he is by bragging about his accomplishments. During your discussion, try to answer some of these questions:

   - When is the first time in the story that the tailor brags about an accomplishment? What does he say?
   - How does the tailor express his self-confidence to the first giant? The king? The guards? The other characters?

Writing Ideas

1. Write a list of the sequence of events in "The Gallant Tailor." Start with the event in the tailor's shop: He kills seven flies with one blow and makes a belt. End your list with the last event in the last paragraph of the story: The guards ran away, and the tailor remained a king. You should have ten to twelve events on your list. Your list may be different from someone else's because sometimes two events can be counted as one big event.

2. Folktales about little and powerless people who get the best of important and powerful people have been popular for hundreds of years. Why do you think this is so? Write several paragraphs about this question. First, summarize how the little tailor got the best of the characters in the story. Then explain why you think people like this kind of story.

3. Do you think "The Gallant Tailor" is the right title for this story? If yes, explain why you think so. If no, suggest another title and write an explanation of why you think your title is better.

Shrewd Todie & Lyzer the Miser

Written by Isaac Bashevis Singer
Illustrated by Carol Hinz

New Vocabulary Words

1. Todie, Sheindel, Lyzer
2. trade
3. shrewd
4. stingy
5. reproach

6. miser
7. cutlery
8. retort
9. strongbox
10. upholstery

11. greed
12. hue and cry
13. admonish
14. apprentices

Definitions

1. **Todie, Sheindel,** and **Lyzer** are the names of the main characters in "Shrewd Todie and Lyzer the Miser."
2. To have a **trade** is to know how to do a skilled job. Tailors and carpenters are people who have trades.
3. A **shrewd** person is a crafty and cunning person.
4. A **stingy** person doesn't like to give things away or to spend money.
5. To **reproach** someone is to blame that person.
6. **Misers** are people who love money, but who act as if they don't have any.
7. Knives, forks, tablespoons, and teaspoons are **cutlery**.
8. To **retort** is to reply in a quick, direct manner.
9. You can store money and other valuables in a locked **strongbox**.
10. **Upholstery** is the material used to cover chairs and couches.
11. **Greed** is the need to possess more money and things than you need.
12. A **hue and cry** is a loud yell.
13. To **admonish** someone is to caution or warn that person.
14. **Apprentices** are young people who are learning a trade.

Story Background

The author of "Shrewd Todie and Lyzer the Miser," Isaac Bashevis Singer, died in 1991. He was one of the most famous writers of the twentieth century. Many of his stories are about the lives of Jewish peasants in the villages of eastern Europe. One of Isaac Bashevis Singer's goals was to make the lives of the people who lived in these villages known to everyone.

Isaac Bashevis Singer was born in Poland in 1904. He decided to be a writer when he was very young. He and his brothers were very active in a writers' club in Warsaw, the capital of Poland. He lived in Poland until 1935, when he left to join his brother in the United States.

When Isaac Bashevis Singer came to the United States in 1935, he had no money and knew only a little English. His brother, who was by that time living in New York, died. Isaac Bashevis Singer was so depressed that he didn't write anything for seven years. But then he began to write again. Before he died he had written 45 volumes of short stories, novels, children's tales, plays, and short pieces about his own life. He wrote in Yiddish, the language many Jewish people from eastern Europe speak.

The story you will read has been translated into English by the author and a translator, Elizabeth Shub.

"Shrewd Todie and Lyzer the Miser" is a story that takes place in a Jewish village in Ukraine. Ukraine, a country in eastern Europe, used to be part of the Soviet Union. Now Ukraine is an independent country.

As you read the story, you will learn about the lives of people who live in the village. You will learn that they drink milk that comes from goats and eat a lot of bread. They also eat borscht, a soup made of beets and served with sour cream. You will learn about the village rabbi. The rabbi is the religious leader who also helps solve problems among the villagers. You will also learn a little about how the people in the village arrange marriages for their daughters and how they celebrate the Sabbath. Most importantly, you will learn about the two main characters, Shrewd Todie and Lyzer the Miser, and how a poor man gets the best of a rich man.

Focus Questions

- For what reasons is Todie called shrewd?
- For what reasons is Lyzer called a miser?

Shrewd Todie & Lyzer the Miser

Written by Isaac Bashevis Singer
Illustrated by Carol Hinz

In a village somewhere in the Ukraine there lived a poor man called Todie. Todie had a wife, Sheindel, and seven children, but he could never earn enough to feed them properly. He tried many trades, failing in all of them. It was said of Todie that if he decided to deal in candles the sun would never set. He was nicknamed Shrewd Todie because whenever he managed to make some money, it was always by trickery.

This winter was an especially cold one. The snowfall was heavy and Todie had no money to buy wood for the stove. His seven children stayed in bed all day to keep warm. When the frost burns outside, hunger is stronger than ever, but Sheindel's larder was empty. She reproached Todie bitterly, wailing, "If you can't feed your wife and children, I will go to the rabbi and get a divorce."

"And what will you do with it, eat it?" Todie retorted.

In the same village there lived a rich man called Lyzer. Because of his stinginess he was known as Lyzer the miser. He permitted his wife to bake bread only once in four weeks because he had discovered that fresh bread is eaten up more quickly than stale.

Todie had more than once gone to Lyzer for a loan of a few gulden, but Lyzer had always replied, "I sleep better when the money lies in my strongbox rather than in your pocket."

Lyzer had a goat, but he never fed her. The goat had learned to visit the houses of the neighbors, who pitied her and gave her potato peelings. Sometimes, when there were not enough potato peelings, she would gnaw on the old straw of the thatched roofs. She also had a liking for tree bark. Nevertheless, each year the goat gave birth to a kid. Lyzer milked her but, miser that he was, did not drink the milk himself. Instead, he sold it to others.

Todie decided that he would take revenge on Lyzer and at the same time make some much-needed money for himself.

One day, as Lyzer was sitting on a box eating borscht and dry bread (he used his chairs only on holidays so that the upholstery would not wear out), the door opened and Todie came in.

"Reb Lyzer," he said, "I would like to ask you a favor. My oldest daughter, Basha, is already fifteen and she's about to become engaged. A young man is coming from Janev to look her over. My cutlery is tin, and my wife is ashamed to ask the young man to eat soup with a tin spoon. Would you lend me one of your silver spoons? I give you my holy word that I will return it to you tomorrow."

Lyzer knew that Todie would not dare to break a holy oath and he lent him the spoon.

No young man came to see Basha that evening. As usual, the girl walked around barefoot and in rags, and the silver spoon lay hidden under Todie's shirt. In the early years of his marriage Todie had possessed a set of silver tableware himself. He had, however, long since sold it all, with exception of three silver teaspoons that were used only on Passover.

The following day, as Lyzer, his feet bare (in order to save his shoes), sat on his box eating borscht and dry bread, Todie returned.

"Here is the spoon I borrowed yesterday," he said, placing it on the table together with one of his own teaspoons.

"What is the teaspoon for?" Lyzer asked.

And Todie said, "Your tablespoon gave birth to a teaspoon. It is her child. Since I am an honest man, I'm returning both mother and child to you."

Lyzer looked at Todie in astonishment. He had never heard of a silver spoon giving birth to another. Nevertheless, his greed overcame his doubt and he happily accepted both spoons. Such an unexpected piece of good fortune! He was overjoyed that he had loaned Todie the spoon.

A few days later, as Lyzer (without his coat, to save it) was again sitting on his box eating borscht with dry bread, the door opened and Todie appeared.

"The young man from Janev did not please Basha, because he had donkey ears, but this evening another young man is coming to look her over. Sheindel is cooking soup for him, but she is ashamed to serve him with a tin spoon. Would you lend me..."

Even before Todie could finish the sentence, Lyzer interrupted. "You want to borrow a silver spoon? Take it with pleasure."

The following day Todie once more returned the spoon and with it one of his own silver teaspoons. He again explained that during the night the large spoon had given birth to a small one and in all good conscience he was bringing back the mother and the newborn baby. As for the young man who had come to look Basha over, she hadn't liked him either, because his nose was so long that it reached to his chin. Needless to say that Lyzer the miser was overjoyed.

Exactly the same thing happened a third time. Todie related that this time his daughter had rejected her suitor because he stammered. He also reported that Lyzer's silver spoon had again given birth to a baby spoon.

"Does it ever happen that a spoon has twins?" Lyzer inquired.

Todie thought it over for a moment. "Why not? I've even heard of a case where a spoon had triplets."

Almost a week passed by and Todie did not go to see Lyzer. But on Friday morning, as Lyzer (in his underdrawers, to save his pants) sat on his box eating borscht and dry bread, Todie came in and said, "Good day to you, Reb Lyzer."

"A good morning and many more to you," Lyzer replied in his friendliest manner. "What good fortune brings you here? Did you perhaps come to borrow a silver spoon? If so, help yourself."

"Today I have a very special favor to ask. This evening a young man from the big city of Lublin is coming to look Basha over. He is the son of a rich man, and I'm told he is clever and handsome as well. Not only do I need a silver spoon, but since he will remain with us over the Sabbath, I need a pair of silver candlesticks, because mine are brass and my wife is ashamed to place them on the Sabbath table. Would you lend me your candlesticks? Immediately after the Sabbath, I will return them to you."

Silver candlesticks are of great value and Lyzer the miser hesitated, but only for a moment.

Remembering his good fortune with the spoons, he said, "I have eight silver candlesticks in my house. Take them all. I know you will return them to me just as you say. And if it should happen that any of them give birth, I have no doubt that you will be as honest as you have been in the past."

"Certainly," Todie said. "Let's hope for the best."

The silver spoon, Todie hid beneath his shirt as usual. But taking the candlesticks, he went directly to a merchant, sold them for a considerable sum, and brought the money to Sheindel. When Sheindel saw so much money, she demanded to know where he had gotten such a treasure.

"When I went out, a cow flew over our roof and dropped a dozen silver eggs," Todie replied. "I sold them and here is the money."

"I have never heard of a cow flying over a roof and laying silver eggs," Sheindel said doubtingly.

"There is always a first time," Todie answered. "If you don't want the money, give it back to me."

"There'll be no talk about giving it back," Sheindel said. She knew that her husband was full of cunning and tricks—but when the children are hungry and the larder is empty, it is better not to ask too many questions. Sheindel went to the marketplace and bought meat, fish, white flour, and even some nuts and raisins for a pudding. And since a lot of money still remained, she bought shoes and clothes for the children.

It was a very gay Sabbath in Todie's house. The boys sang and the girls danced. When the children asked their father where he had gotten the money, he replied, "It is forbidden to mention money during the Sabbath."

Sunday, as Lyzer (barefoot and almost naked, to save his clothes) sat on his box finishing up a dry crust of bread with borscht, Todie arrived and, handing him his silver spoon, said, "It's too bad. This time your spoon did not give birth to a baby."

"What about the candlesticks?" Lyzer inquired anxiously.

Todie sighed deeply. "The candlesticks died."

Lyzer got up from his box so hastily that he overturned his plate of borscht.

"You fool! How can candlesticks die?" he screamed.

"If spoons can give birth, candlesticks can die."

Lyzer raised a great hue and cry and had Todie called before the rabbi. When the rabbi heard both sides of the story, he burst out laughing. "It serves you right," he said to Lyzer. "If you hadn't chosen to believe that spoons give birth, now you would not be forced to believe that your candlesticks died."

"But it's all nonsense," Lyzer objected.

"Did you not expect the candlesticks to give birth to other candlesticks?" the rabbi said admonishingly. "If you accept nonsense when it brings you profit, you must also accept nonsense when it brings you loss." And he dismissed the case.

The following day, when Lyzer the miser's wife brought him his borscht and dry bread, Lyzer said to her, "I will eat only the bread. Borscht is too expensive a food, even without sour cream."

The story of the silver spoons that gave birth and the candlesticks that died spread quickly through the town. All the people enjoyed Todie's victory and Lyzer the miser's defeat. The shoemaker's and tailor's apprentices, as was their custom whenever there was an important happening, made up a song about it:

> *Lyzer, put your grief aside.*
> *What if your candlesticks have died?*
> *You're the richest man on earth*
> *with silver spoons that can give birth*
> *and silver eggs as living proof*
> *of flying cows above your roof.*
> *Don't sit there eating crusts of bread—*
> *To silver grandsons look ahead.*

However, time passed and Lyzer's silver spoons never gave birth again.

Extending Comprehension

Story Questions

1. How do you know that Todie's family is very poor? List at least two details that let us know that the family is poor.
2. What reason does Todie give to Lyzer for wanting to borrow his silver tablespoon?
3. When Todie returns the tablespoon to Lyzer, he also lays down his own teaspoon. How does Todie explain the second spoon to Lyzer?
4. Why is Lyzer so eager to loan his tablespoon to Todie the next time Todie asks to borrow it?
5. Why does Lyzer hesitate when Todie asks to borrow the candlesticks?
6. Why does Lyzer decide to loan Todie his eight silver candlesticks?
7. What does Todie do with the candlesticks?
8. How does Todie explain to his wife how he got the money?
9. What does Sheindel do with the money?
10. How does Todie explain the loss of the candlesticks to Lyzer?
11. Why does the rabbi dismiss the case that Lyzer brought against Todie?
12. Why do all the people of the village enjoy Todie's victory and Lyzer's defeat?

Discussion Topics

1. Isaac Bashevis Singer sometimes writes sentences that have more than one meaning. Read each of the sentences below and discuss its meaning. First discuss what it means in the story and then talk about some other possible meanings of these sentences.
   - "If you accept nonsense when it brings you profit, you must also accept nonsense when it brings you loss."
   - "It was said of Todie that if he decided to deal in candles the sun would never set."

2. Do you think Lyzer should be called a miser? Why or why not? Answer the questions beow, and then decide if Lyzer is a miser. If you don't think so, find some other words to describe him.
   - Why does Lyzer have his wife bake him bread only once in four weeks?
   - Why doesn't Lyzer feed his goat?
   - Why doesn't Lyzer drink the milk from his goat?
   - Why doesn't Lyzer sit on his chairs?
   - Why won't Lyzer wear his shoes?
   - Why won't Lyzer wear most of his clothes?
   - Why does Lyzer keep lending his tablespoons to Todie?
   - Should Lyzer be called a miser?
   - If not, what words should be used to describe him?

3. Todie does not always tell the truth. Would you trust him? To discuss this question you should
   - find the places in the story where Todie lies to Lyzer.
   - find the place where Todie lies to his wife to explain where he got the money.
   - discuss when Todie lies and why he lies. Then decide if you would trust anything he says to you.

Writing Ideas

1. Lyzer had Todie called before the rabbi, who was also a judge. Pretend you are a newspaper reporter who is writing a news report about this event. Write all the things Lyzer accuses Todie of, describe how Todie defends himself, and tell what the rabbi decides. If you write your story as if people are talking, you can get three friends to act out the parts of Todie, Lyzer, and the rabbi.

2. There is a lesson to be learned from this story. The lesson is about greed. What do you think the lesson is? Why do you think Isaac Bashevis Singer wrote the story? Write several paragraphs that answer these two questions.

NO ONE IS GOING TO NASHVILLE

by Mavis Jukes
Illustrated by Lloyd Bloom

New Vocabulary Words

1. stoop
2. conducting a symphony
3. veterinarian, vet, D.V.M.

4. at my expense
5. zoris
6. egg poacher, griddle
7. pound

8. classified section
9. swoon
10. courting
11. hop a freight

Definitions

1. A **stoop** is a small porch with steps.
2. When **conducting a symphony,** you raise your arms and use your hands to lead the musicians.
3. A **veterinarian** is a medical doctor who treats animals. **Vet** is a shorter word for veterinarian. The letters **D.V.M.** stand for Doctor of Veterinary Medicine.
4. When something happens **at my expense,** it costs me something.
5. **Zoris** are rubber sandals with two straps on each side that meet between your big and second toe. Other names for zoris are flip-flops and thong shoes.
6. An **egg poacher** and a **griddle** are used for cooking. An egg poacher cooks eggs that are out of their shells by steaming them. A griddle is a frying pan without any sides.

7. The **pound** is a place where lost or unwanted animals are taken for shelter. The pound is usually a temporary place for them to stay.
8. The **classified section** of a newspaper is the place where brief advertisements are placed. These ads can be for many things, such as help wanted, job opportunities, buying and selling items, and lost and found items.
9. When you **swoon,** you faint.
10. When someone is **courting** you, that person is seeking your affection.
11. Some people sneak onto a freight train to get a free ride. These people **hop a freight** instead of paying to ride on a passenger train.

Story Background

Mavis Jukes, the author of this story, is a lawyer who writes realistic fiction about children.

The title of this story is "No One Is Going to Nashville." Nashville is a city in Tennessee that is known for being the center of country-western music. Nashville is the home of the Grand Ole Opry, a famous music hall that once broadcasted its shows over the radio. Many country-western singers started their careers on the stage of the Grand Ole Opry.

"No One Is Going to Nashville" is about common situations that many children face.

Sonia's parents are divorced. She lives with her dad and stepmother on the weekends and with her mom the rest of the time. When Sonia wants to keep something and her dad won't let her, she calls her mom, even though she knows her mom will have to say *no* to her as well. Sonia is hoping to make her dad feel bad enough that he will change his mind. She is persistent in her efforts to convince him to see things her way. In the end, Sonia finds out that her stepmother, Annette, can be convincing when Annette feels strongly about something.

Focus Questions

- What do Sonia and her stepmother, Annette, have in common?
- Why are the ads that Sonia and her dad write different from each other, even though they are about the same thing?
- How does the story Annette tells to Sonia explain the title "No One Is Going to Nashville"?

NO ONE IS GOING TO NASHVILLE

by Mavis Jukes

Illustrated by Lloyd Bloom

It was six o'clock in the morning. Sonia checked her alligator lizard. He was out of termites, and possibly in a bad mood. She decided to leave him alone. Nobody else was up except Ms. Mackey, the goose. She was standing on the back deck, talking to herself.

Sonia sat up in the kitchen with her knees inside her nightgown. She peered out the window. The moon was still up above the rooftops. The houses were beginning to pale.

There was a dog on the stoop! He was eating radishes on the mat.

Sonia opened the door. "Hello doggy!" she said. She knelt down. "You like radishes?"

He licked her face.

"Have you been into the garbage?"

He signaled to her with his ears.

"Stay!" said Sonia. She went back in the house and clattered in the pot cupboard.

"What time is it, Sonia?" her father called from the bedroom.

Sonia didn't answer because he had forgotten to call her "Dr. Ackley." She filled the bottom of the egg poacher with water and left it on the stoop, then went into the house and to the bedroom. "Dad," she said. "What do you think is a good name for a dog?"

He was trying to doze. "I'm closing my eyes and thinking," he lied.

Sonia waited. "You're sleeping!" she said.

He opened one eye. "Names for dogs. Let's see. Dog names. Ask Annette. She's the dog lover. What *time* is it?"

"About six fifteen," said Annette. "I heard the train go by a few minutes ago." She rolled over.

Sonia went over to her stepmother's side of the bed. "Annette!" she said. "What name do you like for a dog?"

Annette propped herself up on her elbows. Her hair fell onto the sheets in beautiful reddish loops. "A dog name? My favorite? Maxine. Absolutely. I used to have a dog named Maxine. She ate cabbages." Annette collapsed on the pillow.

"Here, Maxine!" called Sonia.

"Oh no," said her father. He slid beneath the blankets. "I can't stand it! Not a dog at six o'clock in the morning!"

The dog padded through the door and into the bedroom.

"Maxine," said Sonia, "I want you to meet my father, Richard, and my Wicked Stepmother, Annette."

Annette got up. "That's not a Maxine," she reported, "that's a Max." She put on Richard's loafers and shuffled into the kitchen.

Richard got up and put on his pants. Sonia and Max watched him search for his shoes. Max's ears were moving so wildly they could have been conducting a symphony.

"Weird ears," said Richard. He went into the kitchen.

Ms. Mackey stared through the glass at his feet and started honking. He opened the door a couple of inches. "*Quiet!*" he whispered. "You're not even supposed to live inside the city limits!"

She puffed her feathers.

"Beat it!" said Richard. "Go eat some snails!"

Off she waddled.

Sonia came into the kitchen wearing white pants and a white shirt with DR. S. ACKLEY, D.V.M. printed on the pocket with a felt-tip pen. She took something from the refrigerator on a paper plate and left again.

"What are we going to do about Max?" said Annette.

"Send him packing," said Richard.

"Do you really think it's going to be that easy?" said Annette.

"Yes. Sonia knows I cannot stand dogs. Neither can her mother. We've been through this before. She accepts it."

Annette turned from Richard. "Well, don't be too sure," she said.

Richard went into the living room.

"Guess what," said Sonia. "Max ate all the meatloaf." She waved the paper plate at him.

"Great, I was planning to have that for lunch," said Richard dryly. "Dr. Ackley, may I have a word with you?"

Sonia sat on the couch and dragged Max up onto her lap. Annette stood in the doorway, looking on. Sonia carefully tore two slits in the paper plate. Richard watched, his hands clasped behind his back. His thumbs were circling each other.

"About this dog—" said Richard. He walked across the room.

"You're gorgeous," said Sonia to Max. She pushed each of Max's ears through a slit in the plate. "There!" she said. "Now you have a hat!"

Max licked her. She licked him back. Richard made an unpleasant face.

"That hat looks great!" said Annette. "Where's the camera?"

Richard began again. "I know you really like the dog, but he belongs somewhere."

"With me," said Sonia. "He's been abandoned. He came to me. He passed all the other houses. He's supposed to be mine." She pulled each ear out a little farther.

Richard turned and paced. "I don't like saying no," he said. "It's harder for me to say no than it is for other fathers because we only see each other on weekends."

Annette opened the closet to look for the camera.

"But," said Richard, "since we only see each other on weekends, I have more reasons to say no than other fathers." He put his hands in his pockets and jingled some change. "Number one: I don't like dogs and they don't like me." Richard pulled out a couple of coins and tossed them in the air. He caught them. "Number two: While you're at your mother's apartment, the dog becomes my responsibility."

Annette looked at him.

"And Annette's," he added. "Anyhow, since you're at your mother's house all week long, and I would have to walk the dog—"

"I could walk him," said Annette.

"—and feed him *and* pay the vet bills—" He dropped the coins into his pocket and glanced at Annette. "I feel that it's my decision." Richard looked at Sonia. "I'm the father. And I'm saying no."

Max jumped down. He shook off the hat and tore it up.

"You call me Dr. Ackley because you *know* I am planning to be a veterinarian," said Sonia, "yet you don't want me to have experience in the field by having pets."

"You're being unfair," said Richard. "I do let you have pets. Even though they abuse me. Have you forgotten this?" He displayed a small scar on the side of his finger.

"How could I forget that?" said Sonia. "Fangs bit you."

"Yes, Fangs the Killer Lizard bit me," said Richard.

"Do you remember *how* it happened?" said Sonia.

A smile crept across Annette's face. She sat down and opened the newspaper.

"I don't recall, exactly," said Richard. "And it's a painful memory. Let's not go through it."

"Well, *I* remember exactly what happened," said Sonia. "You said that you were so fast you once won a pie-eating contest, and that when you were a kid people used to call you Swifty."

Richard pretended to be bored with the story.

"And," continued Sonia, "you said you bet you could put a termite down in front of Fangs before he could snap it out of your fingers."

Richard folded his arms and looked at the ceiling.

"I said, 'I bet you can't,'" said Sonia. "Annette said, 'Don't try it.'"

Richard stared over at Annette, who was behind the newspaper trying not to laugh.

"And," said Sonia, "Fangs bit you."

"I know you're laughing, Annette," said Richard as she turned the page. "Is this my fault, too?" He pulled up his pant leg. "What do you see here?" he asked.

"A white leg with blue hairs," said Sonia.

"Wrong!" said Richard. "A bruise. Laugh it up, Annette, at my expense!"

Annette folded the newspaper. "You were teasing Ms. Mackey, and she bit you."

"Teasing Mrs. Mackey!" said Richard. "I was getting mud off my zoris!"

"Mizzzzzzzzz Mackey," said Sonia. "You were washing your feet in *her* pool, knowing she hates bare feet, and she bit you."

Richard threw up his hands. "*Her* pool. Now it's *her* pool. I built that for carp or goldfish!"

"*We* built that," said Annette.

"For whatever I wanted to put in it, and I chose a goose," said Sonia.

"No dog!" shouted Richard. He stalked into the kitchen, Annette and Sonia following him. "Send Weirdears home!" He crashed through the pot cupboard. "Where's the other half of the egg poacher?" He banged a griddle onto the stove. "No dog! Discussion closed!"

Sonia and Max went out on the stoop. They stood there a moment. Then Sonia bent down and gripped Max's nose with both hands. She looked into his eyes, frowning. "Go home!" said Sonia, knowing that he *was* home.

By the time breakfast was over and the dishes were done, Max had been sent away so many times by Richard that he moved off the stoop and into the hedge.

At noon, Richard called the pound. Sonia and Annette were listening.

Richard said, "You only keep strays five days? *Then* what? You must be kidding! Good-bye."

Sonia took the phone from him. She dialed her mother's number. "Hello, Mom?"

Annette left the room.

"Mom, can you and I keep a nice dog that Dad *hates* but I *love*?" Sonia glared at Richard and said to her mother, "Just a minute, someone's listening." She stepped into the closet with the telephone and closed the door. "Well, it would only be until we could locate the owner." Silence. "I *know* there are no dogs allowed in the apartment house, but nobody needs to know but us!" Silence, then mumbling. Sonia came out of the closet. "I know you were listening, Dad!"

"I admit it," said Richard. "And I'll tell you what. You really just want to locate the owner? Nobody told me that. Fair enough! You write a description of the dog. We'll run an ad in the classified section. We'll keep the dog as long as the pound would. By next weekend, we'll know something."

"Thanks, Dad!" Sonia gave him a hug.

Richard felt pleased with himself. He broke into a song.

Sonia ran to the freezer and took out four hot dogs. Then off she raced to her room for a pencil and paper. "Oops!" she said. She darted back into the kitchen and grabbed a handful of Cheerios out of the box. She opened the sliding door and threw the Cheerios onto the deck for Ms. Mackey. Then she said, "Dad? Will you please feed Fangs?"

"All right," said Richard. "I can deal with the lizard. Where's my leather glove?"

Sonia ran out the door. "Max!" she said. "Here!" She was breathless. "Here!" She fed him the hot dogs, one at a time.

Then Sonia wrote the ad:

*Found. Brown dog with a white
background. Wearing paper hat.
Misbehaves. Has radish breath. Answers to
the name "Weirdears." Call 233-7161.*

Sonia put the paper in her "DR. S. ACKLEY, D.V.M." pocket, and had a tumble with Max on the lawn. They spent the afternoon together, being pals. When it was time to go to her mother's house, Sonia hugged Max and told him: "I'll see you again, so I won't say good-bye."

Max wagged his tail in a circle.

Sonia went into the house and handed Richard the ad.

"Sonia!" said Richard.

"Dr. Ackley," said Sonia.

"This doesn't even sound like the same dog! Max isn't a 'brown dog with a white background.' He's a white dog with brown spots!"

"Same thing," said Sonia.

"Also, Max doesn't misbehave. He's very polite," said Richard.

"Then why don't you like him?" said Sonia.

Richard turned the paper over, took a pen from his shirt, and clicked it once. "Let's see."

Sonia read over his shoulder as he wrote:

Found. White dog with brown spots.
Vicinity Railroad Hill. Male. No tags.
Medium-sized. Strange ears. Call 233-7161,
through May 3rd.

"What does it mean, 'through May 3rd?'" she asked.

"After that," said Richard, "we're going to let someone adopt him."

Sonia fell into a swoon on the rug. "Us," she thought as she lay on the floor with her eyes shut.

"Now," said Richard. "Off we go to your mother's. We're already late."

As they were leaving, Annette picked up Max and waved his paw at Sonia. Sonia grinned.

"Ridiculous!" said Richard. He gave Annette a kiss. "Be right back!"

The week passed by slowly. Neither the newspaper ad nor calls to the pound and police station produced Max's owner. On Friday evening, Richard and Annette sat on the couch, waiting for Sonia to arrive. Max put his nose on Richard's knee.

Richard looked at Annette. "What does he want?" he asked.

"He's courting you," said Annette as Max licked Richard's hand.

"He's *tasting* me," said Richard. "He's thinking about sinking his teeth in my leg."

A horn beeped in the driveway. "Here she is now," Richard said. He went out on the stoop and waved.

"See you Sunday!" called Sonia's mother to Richard. She whizzed backward out of the driveway.

Sonia took the steps two at a time and ran past Richard. "Max!" she said. "I knew you'd be here!"

"Unfortunately," said Richard. "No owner."

"That's what I figured," said Sonia. "So"—she dug in her pack—"I wrote the ad"—she handed a note to Richard—"for Max to be adopted."

"Great!" said Richard. He felt relieved. "Then you *do* understand."

Neatly written, in multicolored ink, and decorated with pictures of iris and geraniums, Sonia had written:

> *Free. We don't want him. A weird dog.*
> *Blotchy-colored. Has ear problems. Tears*
> *hats. Lives in hedges. Wags his tail in a*
> *circle instead of up and down.*
> *Call 233-7161.*

"Sonia!" said Richard.

She pointed to the name on her pocket.

"Dr. Ackley!" they both said at once.

"Nobody will want to adopt the dog if we say this in the paper."

"I know," said Sonia.

"Well, I also wrote one," said Richard. "I've already had it placed in tomorrow's paper." He opened his wallet and unfolded a piece of paper. He read it aloud:

> *"Free to a good home. Beautiful, medium-*
> *sized male, Shepherd-mix. Snow white*
> *with gorgeous brown dots. A real*
> *storybook dog that will be an excellent*
> *companion. Would prefer country*
> *environment. Loves children. Sweet*
> *disposition. Obedient. Expressive ears.*
> *Call 233-7161."*

Sonia looked at Richard and said, "Don't call me Dr. Ackley anymore." She turned and stormed into the kitchen. She unbuttoned her shirt and balled it up. She stuffed it into a box under the sink that was filled with bottles for the recycling center.

Very late that night, Sonia woke up. She slipped from her bed and found Max in the living room. She searched for some cowboy music on the radio. She held Max in her arms.

Annette appeared in the doorway. "What are you two doing up?"

"It might be our last night," said Sonia. "We're dancing. He weighs a ton." She turned off the radio and put Max down. "What are you doing up?"

"Restless," said Annette. "I keep hearing the trains—listen!" She put her finger to her lips. She closed her eyes. A train was drawing closer through the darkness to the station. They heard the lonesome wail of the train whistle. "It must be midnight. The freight is coming in."

Max whined softly. Sofia and Annette knelt beside him.

"I knew Mom or Dad wouldn't let me keep him," began Sonia. "Neither of them likes dogs."

Max pushed his nose into Sonia's hand. She smoothed his whiskers. Annette said nothing.

"And," continued Sonia, "animals are better off in the country. It's just that I really believed that Max could be mine."

Annette didn't speak.

The freight train clattered away into the night. The whistle sounded faint and lost. They listened until it was gone.

Max sat with his neck stretched way back and his nose pointed up while they scratched his throat. He looked something like a stork.

"Max reminds me of Maxine," said Annette quietly.

"Really?" said Sonia. "What happened to Maxine?"

"Nobody knows for sure," said Annette. "She went off one day and didn't come back."

"Oh," said Sonia.

"We lived near the tracks—"

"Oh," said Sonia.

"My father was an engineer. One night he came home looking very sad." Annette's eyes were filling. "And my father told me—"

Sonia clutched Annette's hand. "Don't tell me. You don't have to say it."

"And my father told me that Maxine—"

Sonia hid her face in Max's neck.

"—that Maxine may have hopped a freight," said Annette, "and gone to Nashville to be a country western star."

Richard appeared in the doorway. "What's going on?" he said. "Who's going to Nashville?"

"No one!" said Annette. She stood up. "No one is going to Nashville!"

"Okay!" said Richard. "No one is going to Nashville!"

Max and Sonia got up.

Everyone went back to bed.

At nine o'clock the next morning the telephone rang. Sonia heard her father say, "Between East Railroad and Grant. About eight blocks west of the station. Come on over and see how you like him."

Richard hung up the phone. "They're coming this morning."

Sonia said nothing.

"I don't expect to be here," said Annette. "I have errands to do."

An hour later a pickup pulled into the driveway. Max barked. A woman got out of the truck and stretched. A man wearing green cowboy boots got out too, carrying a little girl wearing a felt jacket with cactuses on it and a red ballet skirt. She was holding an Eskimo Pie.

Richard walked down the steps with Max beside him. Sonia lingered in the doorway. Annette came out on the stoop holding the box for the recycling center. Sonia's shirt was tucked between the bottles. Annette rested a corner of the box on the rail.

"Is this the dog?" said the woman. "He's a beauty!"

"Yes," said Richard.

The cowboy knelt down with his daughter. "Hey, partner!"

Max went over to them.

"Howdy boy!"

The little girl put out her hand, and Max licked it.

"Do you have a yard?" asked Richard.

"A ranch," said the cowboy. "With a lake." He patted Max. "What's your name, boy?"

"Max," said Richard.

"Why, you doggone pelican!" the cowboy told Max. "I have an uncle named Max!"

"We'll take him," said the woman. "For our little girl."

Sonia came out on the stoop. "Annette! Could you ask them about taking a goose, too?" She was blinking back tears. "And an alligator lizard?"

Annette heard a whistle. The train was coming in. "Listen!" she said. "No one is going to Nashville!" She pulled Sonia's shirt from the box. The box fell from her arms, and the bottles shattered on the cement.

"We're keeping the dog," said Annette. She almost choked on the words. She pressed the shirt into Sonia's hands.

Annette started down the steps. "We're keeping the dog!"

"Watch out for the glass!" said Richard.

Annette went to the little girl. "I'm sorry," she said. She picked up Max. She looked at Richard. "We're keeping this dog for our little girl." Tears were falling. She climbed the stairs.

"Okay! Okay! Watch out for the glass," said Richard.

Sonia was waiting. Annette put Max into her arms. "For Dr. Ackley," said Annette, "from your Wicked Stepmother and from your father, with love. Discussion closed."

Extending Comprehension

Story Questions

1. Sonia wants to be a veterinarian. What clues in the story let you know that she loves animals?
2. Sonia's parents don't share her love of animals, but her stepmother does. What do you learn about Annette that indicates she wouldn't mind keeping Max?
3. How do you know Sonia's dad doesn't like her pets?
4. What reasons does Sonia's dad give to explain why she can't keep Max?
5. Why are the ads that Sonia and her dad write about Max different from each other?
6. What does Annette mean when she says, "No one is going to Nashville"?

Discussion Topics

1. Sonia is a clever and creative girl. Use examples from the story to support this statement. During your discussion, try to answer the following questions:

   - How does Sonia let people know she wanted to be a veterinarian?

   - What kinds of pets does she have and what are their names?

   - What does Sonia do when she writes the ads about Max?

2. Annette seems to really understand Sonia's connection with Max. Why do you think she does? During your discussion, try to answer the following questions:

   - What happened to Annette's dog Maxine?

   - Why do trains remind Annette of Maxine?

   - Why does hearing the train whistle make Annette decide that Max isn't leaving?

Writing Ideas

1. Suppose you are a reporter for your school newspaper. The editor asks you to write an article for Career Day. You decide to interview Sonia because you've heard she's sure she wants to be a veterinarian when she gets older. Write the questions you want to ask Sonia and write out the answers you think she will give, based on what you've learned about her from reading the story.
2. Pretend you find a dog that an adult in your family won't let you keep. Write the ideas you would give for keeping the dog. Write the responses you would expect the adult in your family to make to your ideas.
3. Think about a time you wanted something very much and were told you couldn't have it. What did you do to try to get what you wanted? Did you succeed? What would you do differently the next time you wanted something?

Barn Gravity

by Nancy Springer
Illustrated by Keith Grove

New Vocabulary Words

1. pocket protector
2. velveteen
3. Thoroughbred

Definitions

1. A **pocket protector** is a plastic envelope for pens that fits in shirt pockets, protecting them from ink stains.
2. **Velveteen** is a thick, soft fabric made of cotton that feels and looks like velvet.
3. A **Thoroughbred** is a breed of horse that comes from England. Many racing horses are Thoroughbreds.

Story Background

Nancy Springer writes in many genres. She writes novels, short stories, poetry, and nonfiction for adults and children. She loves horses and is a volunteer for Horseback Riding for the Handicapped. "Barn Gravity" is one of her many stories that incorporates her affection for and knowledge about horses.

The main character in this story is John. John knows a great deal about the science of physics. **Physics** is the study of matter, energy, force, and motion. John uses many physics terms throughout the story, as he often looks at things from the point of view of a scientist. Here are some of the words he uses: **centrifugal** and **centripetal force, inertia, impulsion,** and **vectors.** You may have heard of one of the world's most famous physicists, Albert Einstein. Albert Einstein was very smart. Sometimes very smart people are called "Einsteins."

Since the title of this story is "Barn Gravity," it's important that you know what **gravity** means. **Gravity** is the force that pulls everything toward the center of the earth. There is no such thing as "barn gravity," but girls who are tired of hearing John use his physics vocabulary decide to talk to him in a language he's familiar with. So they tease him by giving him a little of his own medicine. They talk about "rearranging molecular structures" and the "application of scientific principles," and have a good laugh at his expense.

Focus Questions

- What is John's plan for meeting girls?
- What things does John learn that aren't part of his plan?

105

Barn Gravity

by Nancy Springer
Illustrated by Keith Grove

"Dare ya," Frog said.

We were walking home from school, the last day before summer vacation, me and Frog Lentz and Bad Ryan Stoner. Frog's real name is John, but everybody calls him Frog. My name is John, but everybody calls me John. I want them to call me something hot, like Flash or Ace.

But they just call me John.

Anyway, Bad Ryan was pushing, like always. He was saying I was a button-down nerd and a science-fair geek even if I didn't wear a pocket protector. Then he said he was going to have a girlfriend before the end of summer, and he wanted to bet me that I couldn't get one. And Frog was daring me to take the bet.

"Bet you ten bruisers," said Ryan.

Being punched in the arm even once by Bad Ryan Stoner was not anybody's idea of fun. I stood still in the middle of the sidewalk and thought. This was a serious bet.

"Dare ya!" Frog insisted. "Come on, John, there's gotta be *some* girl can like you!"

That was all there was to it, too. The girl had to say she liked me and she would go with me. We weren't old enough to date, so we didn't have to kiss or anything.

I flicked my hair back out of my eyes and tried to look cool. "Sure," I said to Bad Ryan. "You're on."

I knew what I was doing. Really. I had a secret weapon. I knew where half the girls in town would be all summer, and it was practically right behind my house.

Mrs. Lynchmont's boarding stable and riding school.

One thing I had noticed about girls, they're almost all crazy about horses. Personally, I could never understand how anybody could like a horse that much. They're all the same. Cloppy feet, long nose, swishy tail. Big deal. But girls think they're wonderful. Lucky for me. I could pretend to think they were wonderful, too.

Next morning I started. This bet of Ryan's wasn't something I could afford to put off till later.

I brushed my teeth and everything, then rode my bike down the hill behind my house to hang around at the stable like the other horse-lovers.

It was just as I thought it would be. All the foxiest girls in school were there, in tall black boots and skinny riding pants, looking just— wow. There were some chunky, plain-faced girls too, but I didn't pay any attention to them. And there were a lot of horses being patted or brushed or saddled, but I didn't pay any attention to them either. Right away I picked out the two girls who impressed me most: Karleigh Reynolds and Jade Ames. They had their hair smoothed back under their black velveteen riding hats, and their eyes shadowed by the brims, and they looked *mean*. They knew me from school, too, and I tried to look cool when they turned around and stared at me. It was hard, because every other girl in the place was staring at me, too.

So I was the only boy there. So what?

So I got back on my bike and got the heck out of there, that was what.

But I came back to the stable in the afternoon. Felt as if I'd better give my plan another try. It was getting hot, so most of the horseback riders had gone home. But Jade and Karleigh were still there, messing around with sponges and brushes and bridles and water buckets. They stared at me again when I rode in on my bike. The horses behind the fences lifted their long heads and stared at me, too. And nobody said hi.

"What are *you* doing here?" Karleigh complained.

I acted as if I hadn't heard her. "Yo, Jade. Hi, Karleigh," I said in my coolest voice while I parked my bike and walked over to them. "Whatcha doing?"

"We're robbing a bank," Jade said sarcastically. Okay, so anybody could see she was cleaning the bits on the bridles, but that was no reason for her to act so stuck-up. She didn't even *pretend* to smile. "What do you want?" she grumped at me.

I shrugged. "I like to hang around the horses."

"Sure."

"I do! I really like horses." To change the subject, I picked up one of the buckets that had a little soapy water in the bottom and swung it up over my head. The girls yelled at me and jumped up, but the water didn't slop out. I felt good that my experiment was working. Science was a subject I knew something about. More than I did about horses. "You know why the water stays in?" I asked, keeping the bucket going in a big circle.

"Who cares!" yelled Jade.

"You jerk, cut it out!"

Karleigh sounded as though she meant business, so I set the bucket down, but I kept talking. "Most people say it's because of centrifugal force, but there's no such thing as centrifugal force. The actual effect is caused by a combination of inertia and centripetal force overcoming the force of gravity."

Karleigh said, "Most people say people who swing things around in stables are asking to be killed."

"By what?"

"By a spooked horse, Einstein."

If she was giving me a nickname, it wasn't the kind I wanted. I wished she'd just call me John.

"You like horses, do you?" Jade put in. She and Karleigh were standing there looking at me, and there was this yellow horse standing beside them with its head over the fence looking at me too, and they all had the same expression. Suspicious, sort of. Like they didn't believe me. It made me a little mad.

"Sure, I love horses," I said, edging away from the yellow one.

"I bet you ride, too," said Jade.

"Sure!"

"You ever had lessons?"

"What would I need lessons for? Riding is easy." I had never been on a horse, but there couldn't be much to it. Just get on the horse and make it go and steer by the reins. I knew exactly how I'd do it. "Getting from one place to another is just a physics problem," I explained. "Whether you do it on a horse or a rocket. Impulsion. Vectors. All it requires is an understanding of the principles of science."

Jade looked at Karleigh and Karleigh looked at Jade and they grinned cat grins at each other. Then Karleigh said, "Right. Fine. So let's go for a ride."

Even though I was making good progress toward getting a girlfriend, all of a sudden I wasn't happy. "Uh," I said, "I don't have a horse."

"No problem!" Jade turned and patted the long yellow head by her side. "Meet Suzie."

I swallowed and nodded at Suzie. Suzie stomped a fly off one big hoof and blinked at me with huge dark blue-brown eyes, and I knew right then my life was out of control.

It turned out Suzie was a horse any rider who boarded at the stable could borrow for a friend. I guess that made me a friend, sort of. Anyway, within a couple of minutes Karleigh and Jade had Suzie in the barn and saddled and bridled and out of the barn, waiting for me to ride her. Those two girls didn't mess around. Next they were putting one of those black velvety hard hats on me, buckling the harness under my chin. I had a feeling it didn't look half as cute on me as it would on one of them.

"I don't need to wear this," I said.

"Rules," Jade told me, but she was giggling. They were both giggling.

"Aw, come on!"

"It's to keep you from busting your Einstein head and spilling your Einstein brains," Karleigh said. "Get on the horse."

"What about you guys?"

"Just get on, John."

Karleigh had a way about her that made a person do what she said. I got on Suzie. It took a couple of tries, but when Jade came toward me to give me a boost, all of a sudden I managed. I didn't want Jade pushing my butt up into the saddle.

Suzie wasn't a tall horse, but she was round. She felt big as a sofa under me. I couldn't get my legs around her the way I thought I would. When I looked down between her fuzzy yellow ears, the ground seemed awfully far away.

Karleigh was holding Suzie's bridle for me. That should have told me something.

Jade pointed toward the riding ring gate. "Take her over there and ride around," she told me. "Don't try to go any faster than a walk."

"Sure," I said. Sounded good to me.

"All yours," said Karleigh, and she let go of the bridle.

I started to gather up my reins to turn Suzie toward the ring. But she gave a jerk of her head, pulled the reins right out of my hands, and jumped into a fast trot, going in the other direction. I yelled and grabbed at her mane, because she was bouncing me around on top of the saddle and I had already lost my stirrups. I could hear Jade and Karleigh laughing, but the sound echoed in a sort of tunnel. I ducked my head. Quick as a hungry dog going for supper, Suzie had trotted me into the barn, into the dark aisle. She made a hard right into one of the stalls, switched around in a tight circle, then stopped where she was with a grunt. I didn't know horses could grunt. Suzie sounded like a pig settling into its own personal mud after a good meal. "There," the grunt said, "I'm content."

I straightened up and let go of Suzie's mane—it was almost white and kind of short and stood up in soft spikes. I patted at her mane with my hands, trying to get it to lie down. It felt warm and coarse and wouldn't do anything I wanted it to. I decided that Suzie was not going to respond to the principles of physics and started to get down off her, but Karleigh came to the stall door. "Stay on her," she said, and she took her by the bridle and led her out of the stall. "Suzie," the tag on the stall door said. I could hear Jade having hysterics outside somewhere, but Karleigh was just grinning.

She led Suzie into the riding ring and closed the gate behind her before she let go of the bridle. "Okay," she said, "now you can ride her." She ducked outside the fence to watch, and Jade came and stood beside her. Jade had sort of stopped laughing, but I had a feeling she was expecting to start again.

Which she did. Real soon. Because when I tried to get Suzie moving, all she did was ooze over against the gate we had just come in. She stood stuck against it like a big blob of yellow taffy, and I couldn't get her moving for anything.

"Kick her," said Karleigh.

"I am kicking!" I yelled. At least I was with the foot that was not squished against the gate. I was getting mad from being laughed at, and I gave Suzie a real good kick. She jumped into that fat-dog trot of hers, and I tried to slow her down to a walk, but all she did was turn a tight circle and come back and press against the gate again, so hard her yellow fur poked through to the other side.

I had had enough. "What is the *matter* with this horse!" I hollered.

"Barn gravity," Karleigh said. "It's the universal force of attraction between horses and their barns. It actually rearranges the molecular structure of the horse. See? Look at Suzie. Her molecules are leaking through the fence toward the barn."

Karleigh kept her face straight, but Jade laid her head down on the fence and howled.

"Sure," I said, grumpy. I know when I'm being made fun of. "So would you please unleak her so I can get down? Thanks for putting me on a horse nobody can ride."

Karleigh looked at me with a really strange smile. Then she ducked through the fence into the ring, took Suzie by the bridle, and led her away from the gate. I got off and turned to leave. When I turned back to see if Karleigh was following, she was on Suzie, riding her around the ring.

I was so surprised I hollered, "Hey! How come she's not leaking toward the barn anymore?"

"Application of scientific principles," Karleigh sang back.

That did it. I knew I had to learn how to overcome Suzie's barn gravity if I was ever going to face the kids in school again, after what Karleigh and Jade would tell them.

"Okay, okay!" I yelled back. "So you can ride the horse, and I can't. I can't ride worth a darn, right?"

"Right!" agreed Jade from the fence.

"So will you guys show me how?" As soon as I said it, I realized I was smarter than I looked. All of a sudden I had a reason for hanging around Jade and Karleigh. I had a better chance of getting one of them to go with me.

Karleigh stopped Suzie. Karleigh and Jade quit grinning and giggling. They stared at me curiously. Suzie stared at me, too. I took off that stupid black velveteen hat, scratched my head where my hair was matted down, gave up on looking cool, and stared back at all three of them.

"How come?" Karleigh wanted to know.

"Why not?" I said, and that seemed to settle it.

They started by taking Suzie back to her stall and teaching me how to rub her down. She grunted at me.

Every afternoon for the next couple of weeks I went down to the stable. By the end of the second week, Suzie had stepped on my feet six times. She had knocked me over twice with her big, bony nose. She had left slobbery green horse kisses on fourteen of my T-shirts. She had puffed horse breath in my ear and chewed my hair. And I was riding her around the ring.

With Jade and Karleigh I wasn't getting that far. They had stopped laughing at me. In fact, they seemed bored with me.

"Every time I try to ride Suzie in a circle, it turns into an egg-shape pointing toward the barn," I told Karleigh. "Every time I ride her in a straight line past the barn, the line bends. It's amazing! That barn gravity warps geometric figures and everything."

"Right, John." Now that it was no longer just her joke, Karleigh was tired of it. But the whole idea fascinated me.

"It really does rearrange Suzie's molecular structure. It bends her whole body. She bulges toward the barn. To keep her going, you got to kick her in the bulge."

"Right, John."

I kept working with Suzie. I got so I could trot and canter on her as well as walk. Sometimes I went down to ride her in the evenings. Mrs. Lynchmont didn't mind. She said nobody had ever paid so much attention to Suzie before. Everybody went for the big, tall Thoroughbred horses.

Sometimes I just went down to bring Suzie a treat, a carrot, a few jellybeans, so she wouldn't think all she was good for was to ride. She got so she would come over to the fence when she saw me, and I would rub her head and smooth down her forelock between those big blue-brown eyes of hers and say nice things to her. "Good fat-face," I'd tell her. "Nice flea brain. Good old airhead."

Suzie started to understand what I wanted when I rode her. When she did the right thing, I would pat her, and she would arch her creamy yellow neck and look proud. Pretty soon I would be able to ride her out on the trail. With Jade and Karleigh, maybe. But they didn't seem the least bit excited when I told them.

One day I was riding Suzie in the ring, trying to trot her in circles that weren't shaped like eggs with the pointy end toward the barn, when I saw Frog Lentz and Bad Ryan Stoner ride in on their bikes. I saw Jade and Karleigh walk up to them to say hi, and just by the way those girls walked I knew.

Frog and Ryan had found themselves girlfriends.

The four of them talked for a long time. I just kept riding Suzie. Afterward, after I had rubbed Suzie down and brushed her dry and checked her legs and feet, and I was just sort of standing around playing with her mane, I asked Jade, "Where'd you two meet those guys, anyway?"

"Huh?" She goggled at me. "At the Rollerway, Einstein! Everybody knows the coolest guys hang out at the skating rink." Then her ride came, and she and Karleigh went home.

I leaned against Suzie's big yellow belly, thinking about my bet with Bad Ryan. I hadn't really done much about getting a girlfriend for a while. I guessed I could start over, start coming to the stable in the mornings again. There were plenty of girls who came there besides Jade and Karleigh. I had even talked to a few of them. Some of them were almost as cute as Suzie.

She swung her long head toward me, and I rubbed the soft fur around her ears. Yellow wasn't really a pretty enough name for the color she was. It was more of a creamy gold, like spun honey. Her mane and tail were even lighter, sort of a sunny white. She had a wide, gentle forehead with a white star on it, right between those big, soft eyes of hers. And eyelashes—she had enough blinky, sleepy eyelashes for six mascara ads.

I stood at the stall door, looked up and down the stable aisle to make sure nobody was around, took Suzie's head between my hands, and gave her a big, sloppy human kiss on her long face.

Sure, I could start making friends with some of the other girls at the stable. Not just the long-legged Thoroughbreds like Jade and Karleigh. Some of the chunky, plain-faced ones. Suzie had taught me not to always go for the Thoroughbreds.

But if that didn't work—what the heck, ten bruisers wasn't going to be so bad.

Or maybe Ryan Stoner would move away. Or maybe I could just tell him the truth. "Sure thing," I would say to him, real cool. "I've got a girlfriend who's nuts about me. You should see her. She's kind of a ditz-brain. But she has this soft, golden hair—and the biggest blue-brown eyes you've ever seen.

Extending Comprehension

Story Questions

1. What is the bet that John and Bad Ryan have?
2. What is John's real reason for saying he likes horses?
3. Why isn't John afraid of riding a horse?
4. Where does Suzie go the first time John tries to turn her toward the riding ring?
5. Where does Suzie go and what does she do after Karleigh leads her into the riding ring?
6. How does Karleigh explain Suzie's behavior?
7. How does Karleigh disprove her own theory about Suzie's behavior?
8. After John admits he doesn't know how to ride a horse, what does he ask the girls to do?
9. What kind of progress does John make with Jade and Karleigh?
10. What kind of progress does John make with Suzie?
11. What is ironic about Frog and Ryan's girlfriends?
12. What is ironic about where Frog and Ryan meet the girls?
13. What is funny about who ends up being John's girlfriend?

Discussion Topics

1. The story says that Suzie taught John not to always go for Thoroughbreds. What lesson does John learn and how does he learn it? During your discussion, try to answer the following questions:

   - Whom is John referring to when he's talking about Thoroughbreds?

   - What does he learn from spending time with Suzie?

   - Does this lesson have anything to do with scientific principles? Explain your answer.

2. John first spends time at the barn because he figures it's a great place to meet girls and win his bet. As summer passes, do you think John still has the bet on his mind?

Use evidence from the story to support your answer.

3. Most schools have groups of students who are considered "cool" and groups who are considered "nerds and geeks." Why do you think students are categorized into these groups? During your discussion, try to answer the following questions:

   - How can you tell if someone is cool or nerdy?

   - Can cool people become nerds and nerds become cool?

   - What do you think about referring to people in these ways?

Writing Ideas

1. The author leaves it up to you to decide what happens to the characters in the story. Pick an ending and write about it. You may want to write an ending that answers one of these questions: Does John get ten bruisers from Bad Ryan? Does Bad Ryan move away? Does John pretend Suzie is his girlfriend and get away with it? You may have another idea for an ending. If so, write about it.

2. Do you think this is a humorous story with a serious message or a serious story with humorous parts? Use examples from the story to support your answer.

by Mildred D. Taylor • Illustrated by Michael Hays

New Vocabulary Words

1. duplex
2. in the doghouse
3. caravan
4. outright
5. lord over
6. spread eagle
7. lurk
8. plates

Definitions

1. A **duplex** is a house that shares one of its walls with another house.
2. **In the doghouse** is an expression that means you're in trouble with someone.
3. A **caravan** is a group of people traveling together.
4. When you do something **outright,** you do it instantly.
5. When you **lord** something **over** someone, you are showing off that thing.
6. When your arms and legs are **spread eagle,** they are stretched out.
7. When people or things **lurk,** they are creeping around and waiting.
8. **Plates** is a short way of talking about a vehicle's license plates.

Story Background

Mildred D. Taylor writes stores that reflect her childhood experiences, both good and bad. Growing up in Toledo, Ohio, she was the only black student in her class during the days before the civil rights movement. Consequently, her upbringing was full of contrast. At home, she learned about love and self-respect. In school and in the community, however, she felt the persistent pains of racism and discrimination.

Mildred D. Taylor writes the truth about American life in the 1950s. She does this because she is depicting an important time in American history. Mildred D. Taylor writes in a manner that makes it easy for her readers to feel as if they are part of the story she is telling. Her stories enrich the understanding of readers whose backgrounds are different from hers. At the same time, they confirm the understanding of readers whose backgrounds are similar to hers. Her honesty and integrity have been rewarded many times over, as she has won numerous awards for her work. One of her best-known books, for which she won the Newberry Medal, is *Roll of Thunder, Hear My Cry.*

The story "The Gold Cadillac" takes place in 1950. During this time in American history, racial segregation was a common practice in the South. Black people did not have the same rights as white people. For example, African Americans had to drink from separate water fountains and they had to stay at motels that were for black people only. Black people were usually called Negroes or coloreds; a black man might be referred to as "boy." Other hurtful labels were also used.

When black people acted as if they were equal to white people, they were called **uppity**. This meant that those black people didn't know their place in white society. Uppity black people were severely punished. Sometimes uppity black people were lynched. **Lynchings** were hangings that required only the approval of a crowd and not the benefit of a fair trial. Many Southern black people lived in terror of being lynched.

The family in "The Gold Cadillac" lives in the North, in Toledo. The two girls are excited about the new car their dad buys, but their mom doesn't share that enthusiasm. When the father decides to drive his car south to Mississippi to show it to his parents, the girls get their first taste of segregation and discrimination. This is a car ride they will never forget.

Focus Questions

• Why is the gold Cadillac so important to the narrator's father?
• What questions does the narrator have for her father and what answers does he give?

The Gold Cadillac

by Mildred D. Taylor • Illustrated by Michael Hays

My sister and I were playing out on the front lawn when the gold Cadillac rolled up and my father stepped from behind the wheel. We ran to him, our eyes filled with wonder. "Daddy, whose Cadillac?" I asked.

And Wilma demanded, "Where's our Mercury?"

My father grinned. "Go get your mother and I'll tell you all about it."

"Is it ours?" I cried. "Daddy, is it ours?"

"Get your mother!" he laughed. "And tell her to hurry!" Wilma and I ran off to obey as Mr. Pondexter next door came from his house to see what this new Cadillac was all about. We threw open the front door, ran through the downstairs front parlor and straight through the house to the kitchen where my mother was cooking and one of my aunts was helping her. "Come on, Mother-Dear!" we cried together. "Daddy say come on out and see this new car!"

"What?" said my mother, her face showing her surprise. "What're you talking about?"

"A Cadillac!" I cried.

"He said hurry up!" relayed Wilma.

And then we took off again, up the back stairs to the second floor of the duplex. Running down the hall, we banged on all the apartment doors. My uncles and their wives stepped to the doors. It was good it was a Saturday morning. Everybody was home.

"We got us a Cadillac! We got us a Cadillac!" Wilma and I proclaimed in unison. We had decided that the Cadillac had to be ours if our father was driving it and holding on to the keys. "Come on see!" Then we raced on, through the upstairs sunroom, down the front steps, through the downstairs sunroom, and out to the Cadillac. Mr. Pondexter was still there. Mr. LeRoy and Mr. Courtland from down the street were there too and all were admiring the Cadillac as my father stood proudly by, pointing out the various features.

"Brand-new 1950 Coupe deVille!" I heard one of the men saying.

"Just off the showroom floor!" my father said. "I just couldn't resist it."

My sister and I eased up to the car and peeked in. It was all gold inside. Gold leather seats. Gold carpeting. Gold dashboard. It was like no car we had owned before. It looked like a car for rich folks.

"Daddy, are we rich?" I asked. My father laughed.

"Daddy, it's ours, isn't it?" asked Wilma, who was older and more practical than I. She didn't intend to give her heart too quickly to something that wasn't hers.

"You like it?"

"Oh, Daddy, yes!"

He looked at me. "What 'bout you, 'lois?"

"Yes, sir!"

My father laughed again. "Then expect I can't much disappoint my girls, can I? It's ours all right!"

Wilma and I hugged our father with our joy. My uncles came from the house and my aunts, carrying their babies, came out too. Everybody surrounded the car and owwed and ahhed. Nobody could believe it.

Then my mother came out.

Everybody stood back grinning as she approached the car. There was no smile on her face. We all waited for her to speak. She stared at the car, then looked at my father, standing there as proud as he could be. Finally she said, "You didn't buy this car, did you, Wilbert?"

"Gotta admit I did. Couldn't resist it."

"But … but what about our Mercury? It was perfectly good!"

"Don't you like the Cadillac, Dee?"

"That Mercury wasn't even a year old!"

My father nodded. "And I'm sure whoever buys it is going to get themselves a good car. But we've got ourselves a better one. Now stop frowning, honey, and let's take ourselves a ride in our brand-new Cadillac!"

My mother shook her head. "I've got food on the stove," she said and turning away walked back to the house.

There was an awkward silence and then my father said, "You know Dee never did much like surprises. Guess this here Cadillac was a bit too much for her. I best go smooth things out with her."

Everybody watched as he went after my mother. But when he came back, he was alone.

"Well, what she say?" asked one of my uncles.

My father shrugged and smiled. "Told me I bought this Cadillac alone, I could just ride in it alone."

Another uncle laughed. "Uh-oh! Guess she told you!"

"Oh, she'll come around," said one of my aunts. "Any woman would be proud to ride in this car."

"That's what I'm banking on," said my father as he went around to the street side of the car and opened the door. "All right! Who's for a ride?"

"We are!" Wilma and I cried.

All three of my uncles and one of my aunts, still holding her baby, and Mr. Pondexter climbed in with us and we took off for the first ride in the gold Cadillac. It was a glorious ride and we drove all through the city of Toledo. We rode past the church and past the school. We rode through Ottawa Hills where the rich folks lived and on into Walbridge Park and past the zoo, then along the Maumee River. But none of us had had enough of the car so my father put the car on the road and we drove all the way to Detroit. We had plenty of family there and everybody was just as pleased as could be about the Cadillac. My father told our Detroit relatives that he was in the doghouse with my mother about buying the Cadillac. My uncles told them she wouldn't ride in the car. All the Detroit family thought that was funny and everybody, including my father, laughed about it and said my mother would come around.

It was early evening by the time we got back home, and I could see from my mother's face she had not come around. She was angry now not only about the car, but that we had been gone so long. I didn't understand that, since my father had called her as soon as we reached Detroit to let her know where we were. I had heard him myself. I didn't understand either why she did not like that fine Cadillac and thought she was being terribly disagreeable with my father. That night as she tucked Wilma and me in bed I told her that too.

"Is this your business?" she asked.

"Well, I just think you ought to be nice to Daddy. I think you ought to ride in that car with him! It'd sure make him happy."

"I think you ought to go to sleep," she said and turned out the light.

Later I heard her arguing with my father. "We're supposed to be saving for a house!" she said.

"We've already got a house!" said my father.

"But you said you wanted a house in a better neighborhood. I thought that's what we both said!"

"I haven't changed my mind."

"Well, you have a mighty funny way of saving for it, then. Your brothers are saving for houses of their own and you don't see them out buying new cars every year!"

"We'll still get the house, Dee. That's a promise!"

"Not with new Cadillacs we won't!" said my mother and then she said a very loud good night and all was quiet.

The next day was Sunday and everybody figured that my mother would be sure to give in and ride in the Cadillac. After all, the family always went to church together on Sunday. But she didn't give in. What was worse she wouldn't let Wilma and me ride in the Cadillac either. She took us each by the hand, walked past the Cadillac where my father stood waiting and headed on toward the church, three blocks away. I was really mad at her now. I had been looking forward to driving up to the church in that gold Cadillac and having everybody see.

On most Sunday afternoons during the summertime, my mother, my father, Wilma, and I would go for a ride. Sometimes we just rode around the city and visited friends and family. Sometimes we made short trips over to Chicago or Peoria or Detroit to see relatives there or to Cleveland where we had relatives too, but we could also see the Cleveland Indians play. Sometimes we joined our aunts and uncles and drove in a caravan out to the park or to the beach. At the park or the beach Wilma and I would run and play. My mother and my aunts would spread a picnic and my father and my uncles would shine their cars.

But on this Sunday afternoon my mother refused to ride anywhere. She told Wilma and me that we could go. So we left her alone in the big, empty house, and the family cars, led by the gold Cadillac, headed for the park. For a while I played and had a good time, but then I stopped playing and went to sit with my father. Despite his laughter he seemed sad to me. I think he was missing my mother as much as I was.

That evening my father took my mother to dinner down at the corner cafe. They walked. Wilma and I stayed at the house chasing fireflies in the backyard. My aunts and uncles sat in the yard and on the porch, talking and laughing about the day and watching us. It was a soft summer's evening, the kind that came every day and was expected. The smell of charcoal and of barbecue drifting from up the block, the sound of laughter and music and talk drifting from yard to yard were all a part of it. Soon one of my uncles joined Wilma and me in our chase of fireflies and when my mother and father came home we were at it still. My mother and father watched us for awhile, while everybody else watched them to see if my father would take out the Cadillac and if my mother would slide in beside him to take a ride. But it soon became evident that the dinner had not changed my mother's mind. She still refused to ride in the Cadillac. I just couldn't understand her objection to it.

Though my mother didn't like the Cadillac, everybody else in the neighborhood certainly did. That meant quite a few folks too, since we lived on a very busy block. On one corner was a grocery store, a cleaner's, and a gas station. Across the street was a beauty shop and a fish market, and down the street was a bar, another grocery store, the Dixie Theater, the cafe, and a drugstore. There were always people strolling to or from one of these places and because our house was right in the middle of the block just about everybody had to pass our house and the gold Cadillac. Sometimes people took in the Cadillac as they walked, their heads turning for a longer look as they passed. Then there were people who just outright stopped and took a good look before continuing on their way. I was proud to say that car belonged to my family. I felt mighty important as people called to me as I ran down the street, "'Ey, 'lois! How's that Cadillac, girl? Riding fine?" I told my mother how much everybody liked that car. She was not impressed and made no comment.

Since just about everybody on the block knew everybody else, most folks knew that my mother wouldn't ride in the Cadillac. Because of that, my father took a lot of good-natured kidding from the men. My mother got kidded too as the women said if she didn't ride in that car, maybe some other woman would. And everybody laughed about it and began to bet on who would give in first, my mother or my father. But then my father said he was going to drive the car south into Mississippi to visit my grandparents and everybody stopped laughing.

My uncles stopped.

So did my aunts.

Everybody.

"Look here, Wilbert," said one of my uncles, "it's too dangerous. It's like putting a loaded gun to your head."

"I paid good money for that car," said my father. "That gives me a right to drive it where I please. Even down to Mississippi."

My uncles argued with him and tried to talk him out of driving the car south. So did my aunts and so did the neighbors, Mr. LeRoy, Mr. Courtland, and Mr. Pondexter. They said it was a dangerous thing, a mighty dangerous thing, for a black man to drive an expensive car into the rural South.

"Not much those folks hate more'n to see a northern Negro coming down there in a fine car," said Mr. Pondexter. "They see those Ohio license plates, they'll figure you coming down uppity, trying to lord your fine car over them!"

I listened, but I didn't understand. I didn't understand why they didn't want my father to drive that car south. It was his.

"Listen to Pondexter, Wilbert!" cried another uncle. "We might've fought a war to free people overseas, but we're not free here! Man, those white folks down south'll lynch you soon's look at you. You know that!"

Wilma and I looked at each other. Neither one of us knew what *lynch* meant, but the word sent a shiver through us. We held each other's hand.

My father was silent, then he said: "All my life I've had to be heedful of what white folks thought. Well, I'm tired of that. I worked hard for everything I got. Got it honest, too. Now I got that Cadillac because I liked it and because it meant something to me that somebody like me from Mississippi could go and buy it. It's my car, I paid for it, and I'm driving it south."

My mother, who had said nothing through all this, now stood. "Then the girls and I'll be going too," she said.

"No!" said my father.

My mother only looked at him and went off to the kitchen.

My father shook his head. It seemed he didn't want us to go. My uncles looked at each other, then at my father. "You set on doing this, we'll all go," they said. "That way we can watch out for each other." My father took a moment and nodded. Then my aunts got up and went off to their kitchens too.

All the next day my aunts and my mother cooked and the house was filled with delicious smells. They fried chicken and baked hams and cakes and sweet potato pies and mixed potato salad. They filled jugs with water and punch and coffee. Then they packed everything in huge picnic baskets along with bread and boiled eggs, oranges and apples, plates and napkins, spoons and forks and cups. They placed all that food on the back seats of the cars. It was like a grand, grand picnic we were going on, and Wilma and I were mighty excited. We could hardly wait to start.

My father, my mother, Wilma and I got into the Cadillac. My uncles, my aunts, my cousins got into the Ford, the Buick, and the Chevrolet, and we rolled off in our caravan headed south. Though my mother was finally riding in the Cadillac, she had no praise for it. In fact, she said nothing about it at all. She still seemed upset and since she still seemed to feel the same about the car, I wondered why she had insisted upon making this trip with my father.

We left the city of Toledo behind, drove through Bowling Green and down through the Ohio countryside of farms and small towns, through Dayton and Cincinnati, and across the Ohio River into Kentucky. On the other side of the river my father stopped the car and looked back at Wilma and me and said, "Now from here on, whenever we stop and there're white people around, I don't want either one of you to say a word. *Not one word!* Your mother and I'll do all the talking. That understood?"

"Yes, sir," Wilma and I both said, though we didn't truly understand why.

My father nodded, looked at my mother and started the car again. We rolled on, down Highway 25 and through the bluegrass hills of Kentucky. Soon we began to see signs. Signs that read: WHITE ONLY, COLORED NOT ALLOWED. Hours later, we left the Bluegrass State and crossed into Tennessee. Now we saw even more of the signs saying: WHITE ONLY, COLORED NOT ALLOWED. We saw the signs above water fountains and in restaurant windows. We saw them in ice cream parlors and at hamburger stands. We saw them in front of hotels and motels, and on the restroom doors of filling stations. I didn't like the signs. I felt as if I were in a foreign land.

I couldn't understand why the signs were there and I asked my father what the signs meant. He said they meant we couldn't drink from the water fountains. He said they meant we couldn't stop to sleep in the motels. He said they meant we couldn't stop to eat in the restaurants. I looked at the grand picnic basket I had been enjoying so much. Now I understood why my mother had packed it. Suddenly the picnic didn't seem so grand.

Finally we reached Memphis. We got there at a bad time. Traffic was heavy and we got separated from the rest of the family. We tried to find them but it was no use. We had to go on alone. We reached the Mississippi state line and soon after we heard a police siren. A police car came up behind us. My father slowed the Cadillac, then stopped. Two white policemen got out of their car. They eyeballed the Cadillac and told my father to get out.

"Whose car is this, boy?" they asked.

I saw anger in my father's eyes. "It's mine," he said.

"You're a liar," said one of the policemen. "You stole this car."

"Turn around, put your hands on top of that car and spread eagle," said the other policeman.

My father did as he was told. They searched him and I didn't understand why. I didn't understand either why they had called my father a liar and didn't believe that the Cadillac was his. I wanted to ask but I remembered my father's warning not to say a word and I obeyed that warning.

The policemen told my father to get in the back of the police car. My father did. One policeman got back into the police car. The other policeman slid behind the wheel of our Cadillac. The police car started off. The Cadillac followed. Wilma and I looked at each other and at our mother. We didn't know what to think. We were scared.

The Cadillac followed the police car into a small town and stopped in front of the police station. The policeman stepped out of our Cadillac and took the keys. The other policeman took my father into the police station.

"Mother-Dear!" Wilma and I cried. "What're they going to do to our daddy? They going to hurt him?"

"He'll be all right," said my mother. "He'll be all right." But she didn't sound so sure of that. She seemed worried.

We waited. More than three hours we waited. Finally my father came out of the police station. We had lots of questions to ask him. He said the police had given him a ticket for speeding and locked him up. But then the judge had come. My father had paid the ticket and they had let him go.

He started the Cadillac and drove slowly out of the town, below the speed limit. The police car followed us. People standing on steps and sitting on porches and in front of stores stared at us as we passed. Finally we were out of the town. The police car still followed. Dusk was falling. The night grew black and finally the police car turned around and left us.

We drove and drove. But my father was tired now and my grandparents' farm was still far away. My father said he had to get some sleep and since my mother didn't drive, he pulled into a grove of trees at the side of the road and stopped.

"I'll keep watch," said my mother.

"Wake me if you see anybody," said my father.

"Just rest," said my mother.

So my father slept. But that bothered me. I needed him awake. I was afraid of the dark and of the woods and of whatever lurked there. My father was the one who kept us safe, he and my uncles. But already the police had taken my father away from us once today and my uncles were lost.

"Go to sleep, Baby," said my mother. "Go to sleep."

But I was afraid to sleep until my father woke. I had to help my mother keep watch. I figured I had to help protect us too, in case the police came back and tried to take my father away again. There was a long, sharp knife in the picnic basket and I took hold of it, clutching it tightly in my hand. Ready to strike, I sat there in the back of the car, eyes wide, searching the blackness outside the Cadillac. Wilma, for a while, searched the night too, then she fell asleep. I didn't want to sleep, but soon I found I couldn't help myself as an unwelcome drowsiness came over me. I had an uneasy sleep and when I woke it was dawn and my father was gently shaking me. I woke with a start and my hand went up, but the knife wasn't there. My mother had it.

My father took my hand. "Why were you holding the knife, 'lois?" he asked.

I looked at him and at my mother. "I—I was scared," I said. My father was thoughtful. "No need to be scared now, sugar," he said. "Daddy's here and so is Mother-Dear." Then after a glance at my mother, he got out of the car, walked to the road, looked down it one way, then the other. When he came back and started the motor, he turned the Cadillac north, not south.

"What're you doing?" asked my mother.

"Heading back to Memphis," said my father. "Cousin Halton's there. We'll leave the Cadillac and get his car. Driving this car any farther south with you and the girls in the car, it's just not worth the risk."

And so that's what we did. Instead of driving through Mississippi in golden splendor, we traveled its streets and roads and highways in Cousin Halton's solid, yet not so splendid, four-year-old Chevy. When we reached my grandparents' farm, my uncle and aunts were already there. Everybody was glad to see us. They had been worried. They asked about the Cadillac. My father told them what had happened, and they nodded and said he had done the best thing.

We stayed one week in Mississippi. During that week I often saw my father, looking deep in thought, walk off alone across the family land. I saw my mother watching him. One day I ran after my father, took his hand, and walked the land with him. I asked him all the questions that were on my mind. I asked him why the policemen had treated him the way they had and why people didn't want us to eat in the restaurants or drink from the water fountains or sleep in the hotels. I told him I just didn't understand all that.

My father looked at me and said that it all was a difficult thing to understand and he didn't really understand it himself. He said it all had to do with the fact that black people had once been forced to be slaves. He said it had to do with our skins being colored. He said it had to do with stupidity and ignorance. He said it had to do with the law, the law that said we could be treated like this here in the South. And for that matter, he added, any other place in these United States where folks thought the same as so many folks did here in the South. But he also said, "I'm hoping one day though we can drive that long road down here and there won't be any signs. I'm hoping one day the police won't stop us just because of the color of our skins and we're riding in a gold Cadillac with northern plates."

When the week ended, we said a sad good-bye to my grandparents and all the Mississippi family and headed in a caravan back toward Memphis. In Memphis we returned Cousin Halton's car and got our Cadillac. Once we were home my father put the Cadillac in the garage and didn't drive it. I didn't hear my mother say any more about the Cadillac. I didn't hear my father speak of it either.

Some days passed and then on a bright Saturday afternoon while Wilma and I were playing in the backyard, I saw my father go into the garage. He opened the garage doors wide so the sunshine streamed in, and began to shine the Cadillac. I saw my mother at the kitchen window staring out across the yard at my father. For a long time, she stood there watching my father shine his car. Then she came out and crossed the yard to the garage and I heard her say, "Wilbert, you keep the car."

He looked at her as if he had not heard.

"You keep it," she repeated and turned and walked back to the house.

My father watched her until the back door had shut behind her. Then he went on shining the car and soon began to sing. About an hour later he got into the car and drove away. That evening when he came back he was walking. The Cadillac was nowhere in sight.

"Daddy, where's our new Cadillac?" I demanded to know. So did Wilma.

He smiled and put his hand on my head. "Sold it," he said as my mother came into the room.

"But how come?" I asked. "We poor now?"

"No, sugar. We've got more money towards our new house now and we're all together. I figure that makes us about the richest folks in the world." He smiled at my mother and she smiled too and came into his arms.

After that we drove around in an old 1930s Model A Ford my father had. He said he'd factory-ordered us another Mercury, this time with my mother's approval. Despite that, most folks on the block figured we had fallen on hard times after such a splashy showing of good times and some folks even laughed at us as the Ford rattled around the city. I must admit that at first I was pretty much embarrassed to be riding around in that old Ford after the splendor of the Cadillac. But my father said to hold my head high. We and the family knew the truth. As fine as the Cadillac had been, he said, it had pulled us apart for awhile. Now, as ragged and noisy as that old Ford was, we all rode in it together as we were a family again. So I held my head high.

Still though, I thought often of that Cadillac. We had had the Cadillac only a little more than a month, but I wouldn't soon forget its splendor or how I'd felt riding around inside it. I wouldn't soon forget either the ride we had taken south in it. I wouldn't soon forget the signs, the policemen, or my fear. I would remember that ride and the gold Cadillac all my life.

Extending Comprehension

Story Questions

1. How does the narrator's father explain his wife Dee's reaction to the new car?
2. How do all the relatives predict Dee's initial reaction will change?
3. Why is Dee upset that her husband buys a new car?
4. Why does Wilbert, the narrator's father, get a lot of good-natured kidding from the men he knows?
5. Why does everyone try to talk Wilbert out of driving his new car south to Mississippi?
6. Why is it important to Wilbert to drive his Cadillac to Mississippi?
7. Why do Wilbert's family and his relatives decide to drive in a caravan to Mississippi?
8. What instructions does Wilbert give his children when they reach the Ohio-Kentucky border?
9. What kinds of signs do the children see and where are these signs?
10. What happens to the caravan when the travelers reach Memphis?
11. Why do police pull over the narrator's family?
12. How do Wilbert and the narrator act when the police start talking?
13. What do the police do after Wilbert pays the fine and is let out of jail?
14. What decision does Wilbert make after sleeping in the car?
15. What questions does the narrator ask her father while walking the land on her grandparents' farm?
16. What answers does Wilbert give her?
17. What are Wilbert's hopes for the future?
18. After returning from Mississippi, Wilbert is shining his Cadillac in the garage. His wife comes out and says something to him. What does she say and why do you think she says it?
19. What does Wilbert do with the Cadillac and why?
20. What does the narrator say she'll remember for a long time?

Discussion Topics

1. Why do you think Wilbert feels strongly about driving his new car to Mississippi? During your discussion, try to answer the following questions:

   - What did he have to accomplish to pay for the car?

   - With whom does he want to share the car?

   - Why is he tired of caring about what white people think?

2. As a child, the narrator doesn't understand some important things that happen. However, when she looks back as an adult, she understands what happened. What things didn't she understand as a child that she understands as an adult? What does she figure out? Be sure to talk about the following:

   - Why doesn't the narrator experience racial discrimination in Toledo?

   - Why do the police in Mississippi treat her father unfairly?

   - When they reach the South, why doesn't her father want her to talk when white people are around?

   - Why does the narrator feel as if she's in a foreign land when she's in the South?

3. After the trip to Mississippi, why does Wilbert leave the Cadillac in the garage and stop driving it? During your discussion, try to answer the following questions:

- What has changed since he first bought the car?

- What is more important to Wilbert than being able to afford an expensive new car?

4. The author wrote this story so readers could have a taste of what life was like for black people in the days before the civil rights movement. Do you feel the author accomplishes this goal? What things have changed for black people since the 1950s? What things seem to be the same?

Writing Ideas

1. Suppose the narrator had kept a diary. Write some of her entries about the following events:

- The day her father came home with a new car

- The day the relatives decided to ride in a caravan to Mississippi

- What she noticed once they reached Kentucky on their trip

- The time the police pulled them over

- The day she walked the land with her father on her grandparents' farm

- Driving around in the old Model A Ford

2. Why do you think this story is titled "The Gold Cadillac"? Tell about why you think the author picked gold for the color of the car. Tell what you think the car symbolizes or represents to Wilbert, his children, his relatives, and his wife.

3. This story has multiple topics. It includes personal issues, such as how a family is pulled apart and brought together again, as well as broader social concerns, such as the consequences of racial prejudice. Think about a topic that is included in the story and write about how the author develops it. Be sure to use examples from the story to support the topic you choose. Then give examples from your own life that also illustrate this topic.

The Hope Bakery

Written by Tim Wynne-Jones
Illustrated by Keith Grove

New Vocabulary Words

1. crotchety
2. spooked

3. belly-side up
4. brambles

5. logging path
6. dappled
7. panel truck

Definitions

1. A **crotchety** person is a crabby person.
2. Something that **spooks** you frightens you.
3. To land **belly-side up** is to land faceup.
4. **Brambles** are prickly bushes.
5. **Logging paths** are roads that logging trucks use to get logs out of a forest.
6. A **dappled** horse is gray with patterns of darker gray. A **dappled** path has patches of sun and shade.
7. A **panel truck** is a small delivery truck that has an enclosed back part.

Story Background

Tim Wynne-Jones was born in England but came to Canada with his family when he was three years old. He has written many books for children, several books for adults, lyrics for an opera and a children's musical, and a number of radio plays. He lives in a house in the country. His knowledge about the woods and the animals that live there is apparent when you read "The Hope Bakery." It also is apparent that Tim Wynne-Jones knows a lot about young people.

The story starts when the main character, Sloane, is five years old, but most of the story takes place when Sloane is twelve years old.

Sloane finds being twelve difficult. He is having a hard time with his school work. Many other things—both at home and at school—bother him a lot.

Sloane's family lives next to the woods. One morning their father sees an elk in the garden. He counts "ten points on its rack." That means he counted ten outstretched points on its antlers. An elk is a very big animal, "*huge,* like a horse," says Sloane, who is trying to explain how big the animal is to Todd, his little brother. The last part of the story is about what happens when Todd decides to find the elk.

Focus Questions

- Why is what Sloane discovered when he was five important?
- What are things that bother Sloane when he is twelve?

The Hope Bakery

Written by Tim Wynne-Jones
Illustrated by Keith Grove

When he was only five, Sloane wandered out of the back garden into the woods behind his house. He was gone for some time and everyone got horribly worried, but he arrived home before dark. He didn't understand the greeting he got when he came back out of the woods. Everyone hugged him and kissed him and lectured him between hugs and kisses about not going off like that.

Sloane asked if he was late for supper. He thought that was what all the fuss was about. Of course, nobody had bothered making supper because they were all out looking for him, and so they could only laugh between their tears and say, "No, you're not late for supper." They asked him, "What special thing would you like, sweetheart? Noodles, maybe? Hot dogs?" Sloane wanted mashed potatoes, and everyone agreed that would be very comforting.

But then came the strange part. At dinner he produced a piece of paper from his pocket with the word HOPE on it. The paper was brown; the word was written in pencil.

"Hope?" said his mother.

"It's where I was," he answered.

Mother and Father and Sloane's older sister and brother all looked questioningly at one another and then at Sloane, who was too busy with his mashed potatoes to notice. The thing is, Sloane was only five, and although he knew his letters pretty well, he didn't know too many words. But the writing was unmistakably his. He always put four crossbars on his Es.

"You were at Hope?" his father asked, looking at the wobbly word on the very ragged piece of paper.

"I thought you'd want to know where I was." Sloane stopped eating long enough to extract a stubby pencil from his pocket. "Good I remembered this," he said. "There was paper there, lots of it." He looked around at everyone staring at him. "Don't you know where it is?" he asked. Nobody did.

Sloane said he would take them there. He tried once or twice, but he couldn't find the right path.

So nobody ever learned where Sloane had disappeared to on that scary afternoon when he was only five. The ragged little bit of paper with HOPE written on it stayed on the refrigerator door for a long time beside the shopping lists, the swimming schedules, the "Hi & Lois" cartoon, the crayon drawings of monsters.

And then on Mother's Day, as a kind of joke, Father had that piece of brown paper framed in a beautiful wood frame with glass and everything. It was hung on the wall above Mother's desk where the pictures of the kids were. And Sloane, if he ever thought about the adventure, never mentioned it again.

★★★

Sloane grew up. When he was seven, another brother came into his life—Todd. So by the time Sloane was twelve, Todd was five.

Sloane found being twelve difficult. Especially school. He was lost at school. He liked lunch and music and geography. He liked maps, liked filling in the sea around continents with a blue pencil crayon. He spent a lot of time at it.

He was upset easily. One morning, waiting for the school bus, Sloane found a dead chipmunk on the front drive and got so broken up about it that he stayed home from school. His older brother, Lawren, teased him about it.

Then one evening, when he was watching television, Sloane saw a lion killing a litter of lion cubs. He wanted to turn off the TV but he wanted to watch it, too. The lion had already driven off the father of the cubs and was taking over the pride, which is what they call a lion family. This new lion didn't want any of the lion's cubs around. The program didn't actually show the new lion killing anything, but there was a picture of two of the cubs crouching together looking very scared. It was worse than a horror movie. Sloane hated it. And he hated himself for having wanted to watch it.

After that, he didn't watch TV for a week. He wrote a letter to the TV station about the show. He wrote about it in his journal; he talked about it with his parents and with his friend Trevor. He even brought it up in class. Everyone agreed it was pretty terrible, but no one seemed to understand just how deeply Sloane felt about it. He couldn't shake it off. It made him ache in a place inside him he hadn't known was there. He wished he had never found that place.

★★★

Sometimes when things go bad, they get deeply rotten before they get better. That's what happened to Sloane. The new place inside him that ached so much for dead chipmunks and lion cubs got a real workout.

In his class, there was this girl, Cynthia, who had something wrong with her. Everyone liked her well enough but nobody really got to know her. She couldn't keep up with the class but the teacher didn't seem to worry too much about it. Cynthia was going to be having some operation; that was all any of the kids knew.

One Thursday Sloane's mother was going to be in town on an errand and so Sloane didn't take the school bus home that afternoon. He hung out at the park instead. He met a guy on the basketball court and they got talking and playing some one-on-one. The guy's name was Billy. It turned out that Billy was Cynthia's brother. When Sloane found out, he stopped right in the middle of dribbling toward the net. It was like the lion on TV all over again. He didn't want to ask but he couldn't stop himself.

"What's wrong with her?" he said. Billy told him. The operation was on her brain. It was pretty major. So Cynthia's family was trying to keep everything as ordinary as possible. That's why Cynthia was staying with kids her own age in school even though she couldn't really keep up.

Billy bounced the ball a few times, watching the way the ball and its shadow met each time the ball hit the ground.

"Like last night," he said, "Mom made spaghetti and meatballs and when she gave Cyn her plate, Cyn said, 'Umm, this looks delicious. What is it?'"

Sloane wasn't sure he had heard right, wasn't sure he understood. "She never saw spaghetti and meatballs before?"

"Sure," said Billy. He bounced the ball a few times, never looking up. "We have it all the time."

Going home that night, Todd was whining a lot and Sloane was supposed to keep him entertained. Mother had a headache. Todd got more and more crotchety and Sloane grew angrier and angrier. He was thinking about Cynthia. How could such a thing happen? At home he got into a big argument with Lawren over whose turn it was to clean their room.

Rachel, his older sister, was making dinner that night. She made pumpkin lasagna. Everybody found other things to talk about. And then, suddenly, Sloane said, "It just isn't fair!"

Lawren thought he was talking about their room. Rachel thought he was talking about her pumpkin lasagna.

"Just 'cause the edges are a bit burnt," she said, and stamped out of the dining room.

Little Todd laughed. He liked the burnt edges.

Father excused himself and went to talk to Rachel.

"I meant something that happened in town," said Sloane.

"What?" said Lawren. "Did you see some more dead stuff?"

"Yeah, your brain," said Sloane.

"Boys!" said Mother.

But it was too late. Sloane couldn't hold back. He didn't want to talk about what Billy had told him. What good would talking do? He wished he had never heard of Cynthia. He wanted it all to go away.

He was sent to his room. Lawren slept somewhere else that night.

The next morning, when Sloane came down for breakfast, the family was excited. Father had seen an elk at the bottom of the garden while everyone else was still asleep.

Although they lived in the country, on the edge of a forest, they had never heard of an elk being seen in the area. Sloane joined his brothers and sister looking out the window. But the elk was long gone.

"I was letting the cat in and the elk spooked when he heard the door open, took off into the brush," Father said. The family kidded him about it over breakfast, but they all knew he didn't make up stories.

"It was huge," he said. "Ten points on its rack."

"What?" Todd asked. Sloane explained to him that the elk had ten points on its antlers. It must have been a big one.

Little Todd wanted to see the elk. He asked Sloane to walk down to the bottom of the garden with him to look for it. Sloane was still depressed about Cynthia and the fight with Lawren. He hadn't slept well and he was grouchy, but he went, anyway.

They went down and Sloane looked out at the forest, seeing nothing more lively than the wind turning the leaves belly-side up and a few noisy blue jays playing tag.

"I found his house!" Todd cried.

Sloane went to look. Todd was crouching beside a groundhog hole in the dirt bank where the lawn slipped off into bramble and prickly ash woodland.

"Whose house?" Sloane asked.

"The elk's," said Todd.

Sloane laughed. "An elk's huge," he said.

Todd poked at the hole with a stick. "Well, some of the dirt fell in so it doesn't look so big anymore."

Sloane laughed again. "No, I mean *huge* like a horse." He could see Todd staring at the hole and wondering how something as big as a horse could get into a hole so small.

"Come on," said Sloane, and he led his little brother back to the house. In an encyclopedia he showed him a picture of an elk.

Todd beamed and grabbed the book from his brother's hands. He tore out of the house and down to the groundhog hole. When Sloane arrived, Todd was comparing the size of the picture to the hole. He looked up triumphantly.

"See! It would so fit!"

Sloane shook his head. "You goof." He grabbed the encyclopedia. "Don't be so stupid!" he said, more angrily than he meant to. Then he headed back to the house to get his stuff for school.

He spent the day being sore and trying not to look at Cynthia or think about spaghetti. He got in trouble twice for not paying attention, once more for not having done his homework. He got detention and had to take the late bus home from school.

As the bus neared his house, Sloane saw some of his neighbors walking along the roadside. They had megaphones. He saw two police cars pulled over to the shoulder. There was another one in his driveway.

He rushed up to the house. That's when he found that Todd was missing.

"He was talking all morning about finding the elk's house," said Mother. Sloane went cold all over. There were search parties everywhere. Sloane could hear them down the old logging path in the woods. "He's never wandered away before," said Mother. "He knows better than that!"

Sloane joined the search. The coldness that gripped him was like a black belt around his chest. As he tramped through the woods behind the house, moving deeper into the forest, the strap seemed to get tighter and tighter.

He didn't usually spend much time in the woods; he hardly ever had. City cousins who visited seemed to think he was lucky to live on the edge of a forest. They always wanted to play out there, to explore. They wanted to look for arrowheads and build forts. That was about the only time Sloane went into the woods anymore. He cursed it now for its rotten wildness, its thousand sharp edges, the pointlessness of it all.

And then suddenly he came to a place in the woods that he seemed to know. Maybe it was on one of those visits from city cousins that he had explored this particular part. He couldn't recall the time. Maybe, he thought later, he had known he was heading this way from the moment he left the house. The cries of the other searchers had fallen far behind, barely distinguishable now from the twittering and screeching of the birds.

An opening. There were several paths leading to it or from it, depending on how you looked at things; where you had come from or where you were going.

Sloane stopped. It was as if he was in a dream. He felt he knew which path to take. He didn't know why, but the certainty of his decision seemed to loosen the belt around his chest a notch or two.

The path he chose led him through the dappled late afternoon into the shadow-making sunshine at the edge of a small meadow. Memory worked in him now. *He had been here!* When or how, he couldn't recall. The familiarity of the meadow was not a knowing thing so much as a feeling thing. As he walked, however, he was quite sure that he had been here alone.

Memory, loosed in him like this, seemed to unbuckle the fear and pain a few more notches. He stopped, looked around.

"This way," he told himself. "There will be an old fence. An abandoned road. A swamp. A junkyard."

He almost forgot Todd. It was as if he wasn't looking for him anymore. Almost.

Finally Sloane saw what he had been looking for, though he could never have given it a name. In the junkyard, resting on no wheels, rusted and overgrown with thistles and harsh grasses, stood an old blue-gray panel truck. On the side of it in faded letters were the words *The* HOPE *Bakery*.

The words *The* and *Bakery* were in a swirly kind of script, but the word HOPE was printed in tall letters. There had once been a little hand-painted picture under this sign: some buns and loaves and a pie, maybe. It was hard to tell now. The paint was all peeling and crumbly.

Sloane looked at the panel truck, letting the shape of it drift into a waiting puzzle hole in his memory. And as he looked, the back door of the truck opened with a loud squeaking and out stepped Todd. Todd seemed almost to have been expecting him.

"You should see this, Sloaney," he called out, waving his hand. "I think this is where that elk lives."

Sloane made himself walk very slowly to his brother, as if to run might shatter the terrifying beauty of the moment. When he got there, he resisted hugging Todd, who was too busy anyway picking up rusted bits of engine parts, a stained hat, scraps of paper. If he hugged him, Sloane was afraid he would burst into tears himself.

"There's plenty of room here," said the five-year-old. Sloane looked around, nodded.

Yes, he thought. Plenty of room.

Extending Comprehension

Story Questions

1. Why is everyone happy when Sloane arrives back home from his walk in the woods?
2. How does his family know he had been in a place called Hope?
3. Why doesn't Sloane ever show his family where he had been?
4. When he is twelve years old, Sloane is having trouble in school. What are the only things he likes about school?
5. Make a list of at least three things that upset Sloane.
6. What does Sloane do to help Todd understand how big an elk is?
7. When Sloane gets home from school, he realizes something is wrong. What does he see?
8. When Sloane starts to search for Todd, what does he find?
9. What is Sloane thinking when he makes himself walk slowly towards his brother?
10. Why do you think the title of the story is "The Hope Bakery"?

Discussion Topics

1. "The Hope Bakery" is a story about a family. The family members help each other, even though they sometimes get annoyed with each other. How do the family members help each other? During your discussion, try to answer the following questions:
   - When does Sloane help Todd? What does he do?
   - What does Sloane and Todd's father do to make Rachel feel better?
   - Why do you think Sloane is sent to his room?

2. Sloane has a lot of problems, both in school and at home. How do you think he will resolve these problems? During your discussion, try to answer the following questions:
   - Why do you think the dead chipmunk and the television program about the lion cubs bother him?
   - Why do you think Cynthia's problems upset him?
   - How do you think Sloane will resolve these problems?
   - What do you think he should do about his difficulty concentrating on his school work?

Writing Ideas

1. Tim Wynne-Jones sometimes writes sentences that make you think. What do you think he means in the sentences about Sloane that appear below? Pick three of the sentences below and write your interpretation of the meaning of each sentence.
   - "Sometimes when things go bad, they get deeply rotten before they get better."
   - "The coldness that gripped him was like a black belt around his chest. As he tramped through the woods behind the house, moving deeper into the forest, the strap seemed to get tighter and tighter."
   - "Memory, loosed in him like this, seemed to unbuckle the fear and pain a few more notches."
   - "Sloane made himself walk very slowly to his brother, as if to run might shatter the terrifying beauty of the moment."
   - "The familiarity of the meadow was not a knowing thing so much as a feeling thing."
   - "Sloane looked at the panel truck, letting the shape of it drift into a waiting puzzle hole in his memory."

2. "The Hope Bakery" ends when Sloane finds Todd in Hope. Pretend you are Tim Wynne-Jones, and you want to make the story longer. Decide what you want to add. You can write about what happens when Sloane and Todd get back home. You can write about how Sloane resolves some of his problems. Or, you can write about what you think would be another way to make the story longer.

Trick-or-Treating

Written by Gary Soto
Illustrated by Carol Hinz

New Vocabulary Words

1. Baby Huey
2. booster
3. restore
4. encased
5. hover
6. incredulous
7. snag
8. menacingly
9. hooves
10. glinting
11. Qué, Mi'ja, ay

Definitions

1. **Baby Huey** is a cartoon character who is a very large baby duck. Because he is so big and awkward, he destroys things accidentally.
2. A **booster** is a person who actively and enthusiastically supports a group, such as a sports team or a school band.
3. When you **restore** something, you fix it so it is as good as it was originally.
4. When something is **encased,** it is completely covered as if it were in a case.
5. When you **hover,** you hang around.
6. When you are **incredulous** about something, you are full of disbelief about that thing.
7. When you **snag** something, you take it quickly.
8. When you do something **menacingly,** you do it in a threatening way.
9. The feet of horses, goats, and some other animals are called **hooves.** Hooves never stop growing and must be trimmed regularly for the animal's comfort and safety.
10. When something is **glinting,** it is shining brightly.
11. **Qué, Mi'ja,** and **ay** are Spanish words.
    - **Qué** (pronounced "kay") means "what."
    - **Mi'ja** (pronounced "ME ha") is a term of affection that literally translated means "my daughter."
    - **Ay** (pronounced "I") is an exclamation. Depending on the situation, it can mean "Oh!" or "Ouch!" and "Ow!"

Story Background

Gary Soto is an award-winning author of fiction for adults and children. He was born in Fresno, California, to Mexican American parents. He grew up without books in his home and without much interest in school. After reading a poem that greatly touched and inspired him, he started his writing career by writing poetry.

When he finished high school, Gary Soto decided to go to the local college and study geography. It was there that he came across the poem that changed the course of his life. The poem he read was "Unwanted" by Edward Field. Gary Soto went on to write many poems and to win an impressive number of prizes for them. He eventually turned to writing stories that generated a great deal of favorable mail from his readers. This support encouraged and motivated him to continue writing stories about the lives of Mexican American families.

Gary Soto's writing reflects his own experiences. Although Gary's family was poor and his father died when Gary was young, he chooses to focus on the positive side of life. He writes about the strength of Mexican American families and describes people who work hard to survive. His stories reveal that, although these families face many different problems every day, they know how to solve them. They also find time to have fun together.

"Trick-or-Treating" is a story about a 13-year-old girl named Alma.

Alma's Halloween night starts out with her going from house to house collecting candy. However, as the night continues, getting treats becomes less important as tricks start to take over. Alma is reminded that there is a scary side to Halloween that she had forgotten about.

Focus Questions

- How do Alma's behavior and feelings change after the incident with the big kid?
- What does Alma know that only one other person at the party knows?
- Why does the story have a spooky ending?

Trick-or-Treating

Written by Gary Soto
Illustrated by Carol Hinz

Alma went trick-or-treating for the first time when she was two years old, waddling from house to house, ducklike, in her diaper. Her two older brothers tugged her along and fed her bites of candy at each stop. She was dressed as Baby Huey, an easy costume because she already had the diaper hanging from her hips and a yellow baby blanket to drape over one shoulder. She shook her plastic rattle, drooled, and smiled at the people who rained candies and dimes in her shopping bag and gushed, "Oh, how cute she is!"

The next year she skipped Halloween because of chicken pox, which she had caught from her brother Ricky, who had gotten the virus from their brother, Manuel, who had picked it up from someone at school. But in her fourth year Alma was once again Baby Huey. People dropped candies into her crinkled paper bag, along with dimes and apples and a couple of bananas. She gave the treats to her grandmother, who in turn gave them to the police to X-ray (or ray-X, as she would say). They were clear of any foreign objects, and the next day one of the bananas, sliced thin so it could be shared by four children, floated in the morning cereal.

As the years passed Alma became even more thrilled about dressing up on Halloween. One year she went trick-or-treating as a princess, with a crown of aluminum foil sparkling on her head. The next year she was Frankenstein, with corks glued to her temples by her brothers and two painted cardboard boxes for shoes. Another year she went as a ghost, which was as easy as being Baby Huey because all she had to do to get showered with candies was wrap her bedsheet around herself and say "Boo!"

148

Now thirteen, and on her own for Halloween because her brothers had left for college, Alma was still thrilled about trick-or-treating. She parted the curtain and looked out the window. Darkness was creeping like a cat up the street. A few toothless jack-o'-lanterns flickered with orange light from front porches. The wind shook the trees, loosening a few stubborn leaves.

"What are you going to be?" Alma's mother asked. Already in her robe, she was filling a bowl with jawbreakers and sticks of gum. Alma was embarrassed that her mother always gave away cheap candy, and never the good things like Milky Ways, Nerds, or boxes of Junior Mints. She gave it away stingily, too. Each kid who knocked on the door got only one candy, never a fistful.

"A football player," Alma said.

"*¿Qué?*"

"I'm using Manuel's old helmet and pads."

Both her brothers had played football for Roosevelt High School and they had each worn the same pads and helmet. Neither of the boys was a good player; they often came home with dark bruises. But playing football had been something to weigh their shoulders down with memory. Manuel, the middle brother, at age twenty-two was already a booster for Roosevelt High, and Ricky, the oldest, who had graduated from USC, sat glued to the TV every Saturday and Sunday watching college football.

Alma went to her bedroom, where she strapped on the pads and then slipped the jersey over her head, working it around so that it draped to the tops of her thighs like a mini-skirt. She pulled on the helmet, the strap dangling like a loose Band-Aid.

"Hello," she said, and the word boomed inside the helmet. She yelled "Trick or treat!" so loudly her eardrums hurt.

Alma returned to the living room just as her father was coming in the door. He was tired from work, and the stubble on his face was the color of iron filings.

"Hey, Dad," she said, bending over in a football stance.

For a minute, he looked at his daughter inquisitively. Then he asked, "Is that you, Manuel?"

"No, it's me," Alma said, standing up and pulling off the helmet. She gave her father a big, sweet smile and then led him like a little boy to his chair, where he plopped down with a sigh.

"I'm going trick-or-treating," Alma said, "I'm gonna skip dinner."

Her father couldn't help himself. "Aren't you gettin' a little too old, mi'ja?"

"It's my last year, Dad," she said, pushing the pumpkin-sized helmet back onto her head. "Manuel and Ricky went trick-or-treating until they were seventeen. Don't you remember?"

Her father didn't say anything. He yawned a wide, sleepy yawn and zapped on the TV.

It was true that all of Alma's friends at school had given up going trick-or-treating. They stayed home and complained that life was boring and that there was nothing to do except paint their fingernails and read their boyfriends' letters over and over. Alma didn't envy her friends on Halloween. After all, her fingernails were stubs and she hated boys. She went to the kitchen and gave her mother a birdlike peck on the cheek. "I'll be back early."

Her mother was at the stove frying round steak. "Be careful," she warned. "Don't eat anything that's not wrapped."

"I won't," Alma said as she left by the back door. Her cat, Tootsie Roll, sat on the hood of the Chevy Nova, a car that had been sitting in their driveway for two years. Her father planned to restore it. Spiderwebs dangled from the tires, and rust spots were beginning to pop up like pimples.

"Hey, you lazy thing," Alma said as she ran a hand through the cat's fur. Tootsie Roll stood, arching his back and yawning, and then poked his nose curiously at Alma's paper bag. She petted her cat and then hurried off to go trick-or-treating.

Alma ran up Mrs. Gonzalez's porch steps in three leaps. She rapped on the door, and Mrs. Gonzalez, wrapped in a housedress printed with splashes of stars and orange moons, unlocked the screen door and smiled.

"Ay, my pretty one," Mrs. Gonzalez said, her lined face bunching with happiness. She reached into her bag and brought out a syrupy popcorn ball wrapped in cellophane, the same treat she always gave. "You gettin' so big."

Alma breathed deeply behind the helmet. "Thank you."

"And how is your mommy?"

"Fine."

"Your daddy?"

"Fine. I'll tell them 'hi' for you."

Alma waved good-bye and leapt carelessly from the porch. She believed that if she crashed, the cushion of the helmet and pads would keep her from getting hurt. She landed with a thud, rolled gently, and got up brushing grass from her jersey.

Alma worked her way up the street, stopping only at the houses where she was sure to get good candy. Her Safeway shopping bag soon became heavy. When she ran from one house to the next, the candies rattled inside her bag and the pads on her shoulders flapped like wings.

"Trick or treat!" she yelled, standing with a clot of little kids. The little kids each got one candy, but Alma grabbed two or three, her eyes always spotting the best candy in the bunch.

Things were different at a house where a man in a dirty T-shirt thrust a bowl of walnuts at her. She took the walnuts, examining them closely, and then looked up at the man. His smile was the smile of a smashed jack-o'-lantern—all but two teeth were gone.

"What are you supposed to be? Roger Craig?" he giggled. His belly jiggled under his T-shirt. His fat son came to look at Alma, who hurried away with a feeble "thank you."

When she was out of sight of the odd man and his son, Alma tossed the walnuts in the gutter, took off her helmet, and unwrapped a Tootsie Roll, which she ate while thinking of her sleepyhead cat. Her face was hot from having been encased for so long in hard plastic.

She looked around. There were few trick-or-treaters on the street, certainly none her age. Most were little kids dragging bags, or mothers with flashlights pointing a safe path for the children.

Alma went from house to house and at almost every stop, she hovered among kids, some of whom were so young they couldn't talk.

"They're so slow," Alma muttered to herself. She felt she was losing time. The little kids held out their bags and looked dully at their treats. Their faces were smeared with chocolate. They were getting in her way. Little brats, she thought, they should be in bed.

But her feelings changed quickly. As she was leaving one house where she had gotten only a stick of gum, she saw a heavyset kid in an L.A. Raiders jacket snatch a bag from a little Ninja Turtle.

Irate, Alma raced after the big kid, who was about her age. The football helmet bounced loosely on her head, and the pads flapped up and down on her shoulders. She ran after the candy-snatcher, knees pumping high, and when she was almost on him, when she could grip his jacket, she leapt and tackled him. The boy kicked and struggled. He tried to smack Alma but instead hurt his knuckles on the hard helmet. And when he tried to knee her, she rammed a shoulder pad into his stomach, which quieted him. The kid gasped and rolled into a ball, groaning.

"You creep!" she yelled, undoing her chin strap and pulling off the helmet. She got to her feet and glared at the little kids who had come running to see what happened. They stood back, afraid. They gave her room, just in case the bully got up and started swinging. But instead he struggled to his feet and staggered off into the dark.

"Don't cry," Alma said to the Ninja Turtle. But tears were leaking from the boy's eyes. His bag had ripped, so the little kid crawled on his hands and knees, searching desperately for the candies that had spilled to the ground.

"Don't worry, we'll find them," Alma reassured him as she stooped to help him search.

"All my candies are gone," he wailed.

"You can have mine," she said. "Here."

She reached into her bag and brought out a full-sized Baby Ruth and a handful of other candies. Without hesitating, the Ninja Turtle snatched them and stuffed them greedily into his pockets.

After the fight Alma didn't feel like trick-or-treating. She walked up the street, cautiously looking around for the bully. She had surprised herself. She had acted on instinct, and her instinct now was to keep both eyes open and her fists doubled. She was afraid that he might be standing behind a tree with a stick. Or that maybe he had gone home to get his older brother. If only Manuel were still at home, Alma thought. She hid behind a tree when a car with only one headlight came up the street. As the car got closer, she could make out four teenagers. They were laughing and playing loud music.

After the car disappeared, after she had gathered enough strength, Alma ran to a house where the jack-o'-lantern out front had its face kicked in.

"Trick or treat!" Alma yelled, trying to sound cheerful.

A woman came out, her face smeared with yellowish night cream. Spooked, Alma nearly jumped from fear at the sight of her.

"Lady—," Alma said, pointing at the jack-o'-lantern.

"This is the last straw," the woman growled, bending down to pick up the smashed pumpkin. "No more."

Alma left the woman to gather chunks of pumpkin and headed toward Sara's house two blocks away. She would surprise her friend, yell "Boo!" and then go home with her bag of treats. This is my last year, she reminded herself, hurrying now because there were fewer and fewer trick-or-treaters. It was getting late and cold. Some people were turning off their porch lights. The wind had picked up and was scattering the autumn leaves. In the distance a firecracker—or a gunshot—cut through the air. It made Alma jump and set her running. She became even more scared when a dog suddenly barked and leapt up at her from behind a fence.

"¡Ay!" she screamed. She ran even faster.

Alma was glad when Sara's house came into view. Lights were on in the house, and she could hear the thump of music.

"Trick or treat!" Alma yelled, rapping on the door. "Boo!" she screamed over the loud music. Alma wanted desperately to be let inside. She yelled again, "Boo, you stupid Sara. Let me in." But no one came to the door. Alma pounded on the door and rang the doorbell three times, but still no one answered. She decided to look through the front window. Cupping her hands around her eyes, she peered in. She realized, to her surprise, that Sara was giving a party. There were kids from school—Michael, Jesse, Julia, and Raul—dancing and laughing. There were pizza, sodas, and bowls of half-eaten ice cream.

"That darn Sara," Alma muttered, upset that she hadn't been invited.

Just then the front door opened and there stood Sara, a basket of candy in her hand. Sara, whose face was made up and who gave off the scent of sweet perfume, said, "I didn't hear you." She looked Alma up and down, adding as she held out the basket, "Gosh, you're tall."

"Trick or treat," Alma almost whispered, not knowing what to do and wondering if she should run or hide her face. She took a Milky Way and a box of Nerds.

A boy from the party came to the door. It was Michael. "Who's that?"

"A trick-or-treater," Sara said. She thrust the basket of candy at Alma and said, "Here, have some more. We're turning off the porch light."

"He looks old enough to vote. You play for Roosevelt?"

"I'm a *she*, not a *he*, Michael," said Alma.

Sara and Michael looked bewilderedly at Alma. Michael peered under the helmet. "It's Alma," Michael said, laughing.

"Alma!" Sara said incredulously. She, too, peered beneath the helmet. "It is!"

They grabbed her jersey and pulled a reluctant Alma inside, yelling above the music, "Look, everybody! It's Alma Flores."

Someone turned down the music. Alma was embarrassed. Worse than that—she wished she could crawl under a rock and die. She took off her helmet, shaking out her long hair, which had become sweaty and tangled, and said, half smiling, "Trick or treat.'

The crowd laughed and shouted back, "Trick or treat!" Alma smiled, feeling a bit better. Sara guided her to a table pushed to one corner of the living room and offered her a slice of pizza. The pizza was stiff and cold, but Alma was hungry for something salty and took a slice that was heavy with pepperoni and sausage.

"I'm sorry for not inviting you—," Sara started to say, but Alma cut her off. "Don't worry," she said, plucking a napkin from the table. "I was with some friends," she lied.

Alma had bitten into the pizza when she spotted the boy in the L.A. Raiders jacket who had tried to snag the Ninja Turtle's candy. The boy had just come out of the bathroom. He took a candy from his jacket pocket and offered it to a girl.

"My gosh," Alma said under her breath. She put her pizza down on the table.

The boy looked directly at Alma. For a second his eyes flashed with hatred. He muttered something, but Alma couldn't read his lips. The boy turned away and joined the crowd by the fireplace. The kids were warming themselves, their hands held out to the flames licking the logs red.

This is terrible, Alma thought, looking around the living room. None of them know about this boy, certainly not Julia, who began to dance with him when the music was turned back up. The couple snapped their fingers and jerked their bodies about to the music. Alma noticed that although the boy was fat, his feet were tiny and rounded, like hooves. Her grandmother had warned her about people with small feet. The boy continued to dance, and with his narrow face he looked like a goat.

Alma squeezed shut her eyes and prayed that this was not happening. She prayed that she wasn't in Sara's house. When she opened her eyes, she could see flames from the fireplace flaring behind the dancers. The flames wagged like tongues over an ancient log.

"This is all wrong," Alma muttered. She looked around the living room. Everyone was dancing, and all their feet seemed small and pointy.

The boy stared at Alma and said something she couldn't hear. He smiled menacingly at her, a fang of light glinting in his mouth. For the first time in a long time, she remembered that Halloween was supposed to be scary, and that devils could appear even on a night when candies rained into paper bags all throughout a quiet town.

Extending Comprehension

Story Questions

1. What are some ways that Alma is different from the other girls her age?
2. What does Alma do when a big kid snags candy from a little trick-or-treater?
3. How does Alma's first encounter with the big kid affect her evening?
4. Why is Sara incredulous when she realizes who is under the helmet?
5. Why do you think Sara didn't invite Alma to her party?
6. After she recognizes the big kid at the party, what does Alma realize?
7. What happens after Alma realizes this?

Discussion Topics

1. Alma has a tough side and a soft side. What do you think the author's purpose is in having Alma be both tough and soft? During your discussion, try to answer the following questions:

   - What things does Alma do that show her tough side?

   - What things does she do that show her soft side?

   - Do people usually have only one way that they act?

   - Does Alma acting both tough and soft make her seem more or less human?

2. Why do you think this story has a spooky ending? Were you expecting it and did it scare you? During your discussion, try to answer the following questions:

   - Which character do you think represents evil?

   - What had Alma's grandmother warned her about?

   - Do you think Alma believes what her grandmother told her?

   - Do you think the author called this story "Trick-or-Treating" for more than the obvious reason? (Hint: Do you feel tricked by the ending?)

Writing Ideas

1. Alma is a complicated character. Think of at least four adjectives to describe her. Describe events from the story that support your choices.

2. Pretend you are the big kid in the L.A. Raiders jacket. Write out the conversation you have with Alma after the party is over. Be sure to explain why you stole the candy and why you stared at her.

3. Alma's grandmother warned her about people with small feet. Her belief is an example of a superstition. A superstition is a fear about something that's not based on fact. Write about some superstitions that you know about. Explain how you think these superstitions got started.

Willie and the Christmas Spruce

Written by Larry Bograd
Illustrated by Frank Ordaz

New Vocabulary Words

1. Vermont
2. staples
3. accelerator
4. gauges
5. hairpin turns

6. lacked the means
7 cord of firewood
8. mudpit
9. navigator
10. sputtered and seized

11. commercial license
12 interstate permit
13. wholesaler
14. rehash
15. deforested

Definitions

1. **Vermont** is a state in the northeastern United States.
2. **Staples** are basic food items.
3. The driver puts her foot on the **accelerator** to increase the speed of her car.
4. The driver looks at the dashboard **gauges** to find out how fast she is going.
5. Very sharp turns in a road are called **hairpin turns.**
6. *They **lacked the means*** is another way of saying *They didn't have enough money.*
7. **A cord of firewood** is a stack of cut wood that measures four feet by four feet by eight feet.
8. *Her life was a **mudpit*** is another way of saying *Her life was a mess.*
9. A **navigator** figures how to get an airplane or a ship from one place to another. A person directing the driver of a car can be called a **navigator.**
10. "The car **sputtered and seized** before it stopped" means the car made funny noises and shook before it stopped.
11. You would have to purchase a **commercial license** if you wanted to sell Christmas trees.
12. You would have to purchase an **interstate permit** if you took the Christmas trees to sell in a different state.
13. A **wholesaler** is someone who sells large quantities of things. Most stores get their goods from wholesalers.
14. To **rehash** a story means to go over it again.
15. An area is **deforested** when all its trees are cut down.

Story Background

The author of "Willie and the Christmas Spruce," Larry Bograd, grew up in Colorado, but this story takes place in Vermont and Massachusetts. Vermont is known for its cold winters. There is a lot of snow, and it is very cold.

Vermont is also known for the many beautiful trees in its forests. These trees can be divided into two classes: **deciduous trees** and **evergreen trees.** Both deciduous trees and evergreen trees grow in Vermont forests.

Deciduous trees lose their leaves at the end of the growing season and grow new leaves at the beginning of the next growing season. There are many types of deciduous trees—for example, **birch trees, elm trees,** and **maple trees.**

Evergreen trees are just like their name—they keep their green needles all year long. There are also many types of evergreen trees—for example, **spruce trees, pine trees,** and **Douglas fir trees.**

Maple trees are deciduous trees that provide something that Vermont is well know for—maple syrup. **Maple syrup** is made from the sap of maple trees. **Sap** is the watery fluid that circulates through growing plants. Vermont farmers harvest the sap from their maple trees twice a year. They boil this sap until it turns into syrup. Then they put the syrup in bottles and cans and sell it so that people can have maple syrup to pour over their pancakes and waffles.

In Vermont, early spring and late fall are called the **sugaring seasons.** The sap of the maple trees is sweetest in early spring, at the very beginning of the growing season. But the farmers also harvest sap at the end of the growing season, in the late fall.

The narrator of "Willie and the Christmas Spruce" is the main character, Willie.

Focus Questions

- In what ways do you learn that the Johnston family is having trouble earning enough money to live on?
- How do the members of the Johnston family help each other?

Willie and the Christmas Spruce

Written by Larry Bograd
Illustrated by Frank Ordaz

That year, the frost and snow came early. We dug our way out of four heavy storms before Thanksgiving. People with time and money were talking of skiing. "The best conditions in years." Not for us, though.

We lived on a northern Vermont farm, the four of us Johnstons, plus my older sister Kate's baby daughter. Which meant we got by with selling fresh milk, potatoes, homemade cheese, and maple syrup.

The best time to harvest sap to be turned into maple syrup is the spring. Usually in late March or early April, when the days are warm enough for the sap to flow up from maple tree roots to the trunks.

And there's a second, shorter sugaring season in the fall. The sap in the fall is not as sweet as in the spring. Still, to pay for our Christmas and to get us through the winter, we had looked forward to a good fall run: our farm shipping out enough syrup to soak thousands and thousands of pancakes and waffles, and we Johnstons seeing just enough profit to make it till the spring thaw.

But that year the early and hard cold stopped the flow of sap. The short fall sugaring season was the worst in memory.

"Stupid frost," Kate said, driving with Dad and me and the few cases of fall syrup we had originally kept for ourselves. It was the week before Christmas, and Dad's buyer had called in a panic.

"Nothing we can do to change the weather," Dad said.

"Oh, like acid rain is just a myth," Kate responded. "Like the hole in the ozone won't get any larger."

Kate's sarcasm had become edgier since she had returned home a single mom. I was too tired to remind her that not everything was Dad's fault. If anyone did, I was the one who had reason to complain. Not only was I sharing my room with Kate again, but we were now sharing it with her ten-month-old baby, Shelly, who cried at night.

We were delivering our syrup, all six cartons, to the wholesaler in White River Junction. The wholesaler reported a bad fall sugaring season all around. The fancy retailers in tourist towns were screaming for additional shipments. He paid Dad in cash and wished us a merry Christmas. The times we had money, we'd stay for some Chinese food in a shopping-mall restaurant off Interstate 91. That day, however, we had orders from Mom to stock up on staples and return straight home.

"Did you even make expenses this year?" Kate asked Dad as we loaded sacks of feed, bags of dry groceries, cartons of baby formula, needed hardware, and loaves of hard salami into the old pickup truck. We'd just spent what money the wholesaler had given us. "Come on, Dad, tell the truth."

"What with replacing a broken vacuum pump and replacing the roof on the syrup house, with hiring an extra man, given all the repairs—no."

No sooner had we left White River Junction than the truck started to act up. Kate had the accelerator down, but the pickup, choking every few minutes, could barely maintain a speed of forty miles per hour on Interstate 91.

"Better get off the highway," Dad told her, "and take U.S. 5 in case we need help."

Although this would add an hour to our drive north, I didn't mind. I liked the old two-lane road that followed the course of the Connecticut River. Watching the dashboard gauges, Kate drove us through a dozen New England towns with their steepled white churches, village greens, and country stores. Past East Thetford and Fairlee, Bradford and Wells River, toward St. Johnsbury. The road was clear but icy and dangerous. The limbs of bare birch trees were coated with crusty week-old snow. The river, a frozen gray, like trapped smoke, looked so cold that I wondered how fish could survive.

"The cost of being alive is simply so high." Dad sighed, his hands slumped in his lap. We'd been silent for most of the ride. I'd thought that he'd been napping. "Truck going to make it?" he asked Kate.

"It could use some new spark plugs," she said.

"Truck could use a major tune-up," Dad said, offering a grin.

"We could use a whole new truck," I tried, and the two of them laughed.

Dad, feeling better, put his arm around me. Pretty soon we'd turn off on our road. Not the state's road. Not the county's. *Our* road. Then up the hill, assuming Kate—and the truck—managed a wicked hairpin turn. Then straight for the lights of our two-century-old stone farmhouse.

I had lived nowhere but that farm in Vermont. In fact, in all my eleven years I'd been to Boston a very few times, but never anyplace bigger. We lacked the means to go elsewhere.

Our farm had been our family's for four generations. I suppose my folks had enjoyed a few good years when I was young. I remember new clothes and a shiny red tricycle. But at least since I'd started first grade, times had been hard and recently had become much worse.

Dad glanced at me. "Willie, maybe next Christmas for those new snowshoes."

"Hey, Willie, trust me," Kate said, tapping my leg for attention. "Given this family's luck with money, you'll be lucky to see those snowshoes for Christmas Year 2093."

My nineteen-year-old sister Kate hated being home again, even with Mom getting stuck in the house with baby Shelly while Kate looked for a job. For all her effort, there were no jobs. Not in our town. Not anywhere close.

Being eight years younger, I grew up almost a doll to Kate. She helped bathe me and no doubt changed plenty of diapers. She taught me "Patty cake, patty cake, baker's man…" She helped me learn to ice-skate backward on our frozen farm pond. She read to me the one summer she loved books better than boys.

But by the time she turned fifteen, it seemed like I rarely saw her. Always scampering off to meet friends. Always close to our mom but having loads of harsh words with Dad. Particularly about boys. Time and again, she warned me about letting our folks stick me with the farm.

The road leveled. We approached our bright-windowed house. With luck, we'd unload the supplies and sit down to warm food before it got really dark.

Dad looked across the road at the group of spruce trees growing at the crest of a snowy rise. "Willie, tomorrow you and me need to pick out a tree to bring inside."

It was a family tradition that one of our spruces served as the Christmas tree, decorated with ornaments collected by my mother and by Grammie before her. Ornaments in honor of children's births. Tiny wooden figurines dangling from hooked wire. Fragile colored glass the thinness of paper. In town we never saw trees as lovely as our spruce.

"Is it okay for me to have an idea?" I asked when Kate turned off the truck engine.

"There's a first time for everything," she joked.

"What's on your mind, son?" Dad asked.

"Well, maybe there's some money in the spruces," I said, ready to be hailed a genius.

"Don't you know, money doesn't grow on trees," Kate said, ever the smart mouth.

"Son, go ahead," Dad said, eyeing Kate to mind herself.

"Well, Christmas trees in town fetch thirty dollars apiece," I said. "Bet in Boston they'd sell even higher."

Dad sat there and considered. Kate stared at me like suddenly her younger brother had actually displayed some intelligence.

"Your mother would never allow it," Dad finally said. "I'm needed around here, and don't even think about going yourself, Kate. No way we're sending a young woman out alone with an old truck."

But, amazingly, Mom thought it a wonderful solution. Providing that Kate had some escort. Someone to watch over her and make sure the money got home. I could hear Mom and Dad talking it out late that night. Long after the last log had been added to the cast iron stove. I could hear them because I lay awake, woken by Shelly's mucus-thick coughs.

It was a rule not to disturb them unless convinced of a prowler or bleeding to death. Not that my parents seemed to do much but wear socks to bed and watch TV. Still, figuring that the lack of family finances was an emergency, I threw back my covers.

"Mom, Dad, can I come in?" I asked meekly outside their door.

"Is the baby okay?" Mom asked.

"Kate's been up with her a few times," I reported.

"Son, you can't sleep," Dad said. He was pretty good at stating the obvious.

"Mom, Dad," I said, entering, "how about if I go along with Kate to sell the trees in Boston?"

Mom gestured me over. Her skin smelled of lotion. Her flannel nightgown looked silly but warm. She wanted a hug before sending me back to bed. Before saying, "Very well. Now understand that your dad and I letting you two go to Boston is a one-time thing. Hear? So be extra careful and keep your purpose in front of you."

In the morning, after tending the cows and hens, splitting another three cords of firewood, my arms and back stiff and sore, I helped Dad cut down the spruces. Another frigid, cloudy day. Except for our bright-orange vests, the colors were gray and dull white.

We left the pickup on the snow-packed road, not daring to get it stuck. We walked from there, leaving quick, deep boot prints in the hillside snow. Dad carried the two-man saw. Not casually over his shoulder, but low, in one hand, serious.

"Shame about these trees," he said.

"Come spring, we can plant something new," I offered.

We worked the saw. Back and forth. Smooth. Working as a team. For the first time ever, I did most of the effort. Either I was growing stronger or Dad was getting much older.

The first tree cracked and dropped, shaking its blue-green short needles free from snow.

"Figure that's an eighty-dollar tree in Beantown," Dad said.

Bent low, sawing just above the snowline, we felled another tree.

"Tell them these are grown in Vermont, U.S.A. —not trucked in from Canada," he said.

"Okay, Dad."

Another tree fell. The wind, kicking up, soon took care of loose needles and sawdust. Another spruce cracked and dropped, and another. The truck bed was filling and we didn't stop for lunch.

It was dark by the time we cleared the last spruce. The bootsteps we had left hours earlier had grown brittle as we traced them back to the truck and drove home. With Dad's help, I took one spruce off the truck, which we would decorate that night after supper.

Mother insisted I take a bath before bed. She didn't want any Bostonian thinking her boy was a slob. The bath itself was glorious. Hot and soothing. Enough steam to fight off the airy chill. It was the first time in a week that I'd fully taken off my long johns.

Sent to bed, I couldn't sleep until Kate and our parents had a long last tug-of-war over the mudpit that was my sister's life. When she came in crying, I pretended I was already asleep. She lifted Shelly from the crib and moved to the rocking chair. There Kate sang a lullaby that put both the baby and me to sleep.

Wasting no time the next morning, Kate woke me early. "Come on, Willie. Mom and Dad want us home before supper."

Way before sunrise. "Can't I sleep just a little more?"

She handed me my corduroy pants and a clean flannel shirt.

As I dressed and tried to wake up, Kate lifted a sleepy, snotty Shelly from the crib. In the dim, chilly room, Kate carried her daughter to the rocking chair. Then she pulled the blanket there around the two of them. Feeding the baby a warmed bottle, Kate softly sang:

"Hush - a - bye,
Don't you cry.
Go to sleep, my little baby.
And when you wake
You shall take
All the pretty little ponies...."

"Isn't she special?" Kate asked me. "I hate seeing her sick." She had Shelly against her chest, burping her.

"She's special," I said, buttoning my cuffs. "Okay, I'm ready." Kate gently put Shelly back in her crib.

We didn't bother waking our parents. The cold as we walked to the truck snapped me alert.

We drove with headlights for the first two hours. Almost no traffic heading south on U.S. 5 except for all-night rigs and a few locals either getting home or leaving to an early work shift. Crossing the Connecticut River at Wells River and into New Hampshire, we drove through the snowy White Mountains just as the sun gave them shape, getting on I-93 south near Lincoln. The radio began to pick up a rock station from Concord. Kate cranked the volume loud and I didn't mind.

The truck seemed all right, even on the interstate. The sky was clear of clouds. We stopped for a quick lunch in Derry, almost to the Massachusetts state line.

Back behind the wheel with an hour or so yet to go, Kate looked exhausted. "Sorry I'm not old enough to drive," I told her.

"I don't mind the driving," she said with a shrug.

"Then what?" I asked, hoping Kate would tell me.

She sighed. "I can handle that I made a mess of my life. But I hate doing the same to Shelly. She's not even a year old. Can't even afford to buy her a Christmas gift."

"She's so young, she won't remember," I offered.

"Hurts all the same," Kate said, "because *I'll* remember."

We were quiet for miles. The number and hurry of cars, vans, and trucks passing us almost put me in a trance.

"So, how many trees we end up with?" Kate asked. She was changing the subject. Which was okay with me.

"Twenty-five decent ones," I said.

"All six-footers?"

I nodded. "Dad figured eighty bucks a tree. So that's"—I was pretty good at math—"two thousand dollars!"

"Not bad for a day's outing," Kate said, impressed. "I figure we give eighteen hundred back to Mom and Dad and keep the rest. One hundred dollars apiece."

This was a lot of money. Like a full year's allowance.

"What if we get even more for the trees?" I said. "Like a hundred, two hundred each!"

"Maybe this Christmas will be good, after all," Kate said, smiling at me.

"You know my best memory of Christmas?" I said. "How we'd go eat too much food in town. Run around with all the cousins. Eat too many sweets and talk to grown-ups. Then fall asleep on the long drive home. You and me in the backseat, like mummies in our snowsuits. Getting carried inside the house by Mom or Dad. And waking up warm in our own bed."

Kate nodded. "I remember."

Before we knew it we saw our first sign for Boston. I had a road map opened on my lap, but the choices were coming too quickly "What did that sign say?" I asked.

"Route One and Tobin Bridge!" Kate shouted. She was losing patience with her navigator. "Willie, do we want it or not?"

"No…yes. I don't know. Better get off."

Kate did so, only to be confronted with another quick decision. "Storrow Drive. Cambridge. Downtown. Willie?"

"Try Storrow Drive, Cambridge," I said, making a guess.

Kate had to do some aggressive driving, ignoring the honks and threats of other drivers, to try and get over to the left-hand lane to exit. Just then, a delivery van sped and cut her off, nearly causing a wreck.

"Jerk!" Having no choice, Kate took the next exit, and we found ourselves near Haymarket and Faneuil Hall, a mess of twisting streets crammed with cars and pedestrians and mounds of cleared snow.

"At least there's a lot of people," I said. At first I thought a hockey game or movie had let out. Then I realized just how many people—and different ones—were crammed together. I saw more people in that first hour in Boston than I had in my entire previous life. All bundled against the cold wind blowing off the harbor.

"And nowhere to park," Kate snapped back. She turned left, then left again, and we found ourselves in the North End, a hopeless maze of narrow, one-way streets. Cars double-parked to let passengers off in front of Italian restaurants and shops. "Look, isn't that Paul Revere's church?" I asked.

"We're here on business," Kate reminded me.

Somehow we found ourselves crossing the Charles River and heading into Cambridge. "Finally," Kate said. "Let's get to Harvard Square."

After getting directions at a service station, we found Massachusetts Avenue and followed it into Harvard Square, where a mass transit station, stores, and the famous university met.

Finding a parking place on Bedford Street, Kate went to phone our parents, while I unloaded the trees. I leaned them against trash cans, against short metal fences, against No Parking signs and apartment building walls.

"Hey! Are these your trees?"

Our first customer!

"Make me an offer," I told a young man in wire-rimmed glasses and a ski parka.

"I'm not interested in buying a tree," the guy said snootily. "I'm interested in why you're deforesting our planet."

"First off," I heard Kate say, approaching us from the back, "these trees are from our farm. We cut down a total of twenty-five. Which is probably a lot less than you waste in a given year. And secondly, we need the money. So if you don't like it, just move on!"

"Oh. Okay, I'm sorry," the young man said. "Listen, you won't have much luck here. Most of the students are already home on break. Go into Boston and try Back Bay or along Beacon Street."

So I reloaded the trees and we headed off. We were a mile or so from Harvard when the truck sputtered and seized.

"What the—?" Kate began to say. But before she could finish, the truck died. "Stay here," she instructed me. "I'm going to find a garage."

Sitting there, Kate already gone a half hour or longer, I felt like crying. But what would that help? So I decided I might as well get out and drum up some business. Boy, I thought, will Kate be impressed if she returns to find that I'd sold a tree or two. And sure enough, as if a prayer answered, a slick-haired man wearing a long overcoat slowed to admire the trees.

"Hey, sir, aren't these great-looking trees?" I said, moving in place to stay warm. "Cut just yesterday on our Vermont farm. Every one a beauty!"

"You talk to Tony?" he asked, keeping his hands in his coat pockets.

"Tony?" I asked.

"Where you from?" the man asked.

"Vermont," I answered. "Is there a problem?"

"Are you supposed to be here? On this block?" he asked, confronting me.

"Mister, I don't want any trouble," I said, holding up my hands.

"Well, we control this part of the territory," he said. "And we don't appreciate outsiders thinking they can sneak in and sell trees. Now I'll give you the benefit of the doubt. Which means you have fifteen minutes to get out of here."

Luckily, Kate and a tow truck arrived in ten minutes.

"Boy, what a place to live," I muttered as the operator lifted our truck up behind his.

"Maybe the farm isn't such a bad place," Kate said. "And get this— I sweet-talked this guy and he'll fix our truck, if it's nothing too serious, in exchange for a tree of his choice."

A new set of spark plugs, an adjustment of the timing belt, and new air and oil filters, and we were back on the road, if one tree less. Unfortunately, it was nearly dark. No way would we get home as planned. Following Memorial Drive and crossing the Charles River, we found ourselves in a ritzy part of Boston. People were heading into expensive shops and fancy cafes.

Miraculously, Kate found a place to park, and I jumped out and took down only one tree. A nice, full spruce. One tree, in case we had to move on in a hurry.

Staying in the cab, Kate motioned me to stop the first rich-looking person. Which I did.

"Want to buy this gorgeous tree?" I asked a woman in an ankle-length fur coat. The strange-looking dog she was walking wore a legless sweater.

"Where did you get it?" the lady asked. She stopped as her dog sniffed a mountain of bloated trash bags.

"From my family's farm," I said. "In Vermont."

"What's wrong with it?" she asked, eyeing the perfect spruce.

"Nothing. It's a beautiful, healthy tree," I said. "Freshly cut just yesterday. Here. Feel how soft the needles are."

"Well, how do I know it doesn't have worms? Or that it wasn't sprayed with some cancer-causing pesticide?"

"We wouldn't do that," I assured her. "We got dairy cattle. Which means we don't spray our land with anything harmful. And it's a healthy tree. I guarantee it."

"To tell you the truth, with all I have to do, we haven't gotten our tree yet," the lady said, sounding interested. "Do you deliver?"

"Yes, ma'am. That's my sister in the truck."

"It is a lovely tree. Promise me that it wasn't stolen."

"I promise. My dad says it's worth eighty dollars," I said, trying to land a sale.

"Do you take credit cards?" she asked. I shook my head no. "A check with a guarantee bank card?" she then asked.

"Sure," I said, not sure. "A check will be fine. Make it out to—"

Just then, a police officer interrupted, "Got a license, son?"

"A license?" I repeated, unsure. "My sister has a driver's license."

The lady returned her checkbook to her purse. "I'm sorry," she said. "But I need to get my dog home." With that, she hurried off.

"Lady! Lady!" I called, following her down the street, only to be ignored. Returning to the truck, I kicked the bumper, not caring that I hurt my foot. "Now look what you did!" I shouted before realizing I was talking with a cop.

Kate, though, saw what was happening and was out of the cab in a snap, stepping between the officer and me. "What seems to be the problem?" she asked.

"Miss, I need to see your commercial license," the officer said, keeping his calm. Inspecting the trees, he asked, "Where are the tags? The interstate permits? You can't simply set up a business in Boston without first obtaining the proper papers.

"Officer, please," Kate said. "We didn't know. Please let us sell our trees."

"Please, mister," I chimed in.

The cop stared at me, then at Kate, then at our truck still loaded with trees. "Well…" he said with a grin, "it's nearly Christmas. Tell you what. Just make sure that you two are gone by the time I return in an hour."

"Thanks. Thanks a lot."

For the next fifty-five minutes Kate and I worked like crazy. Ringing doorbells. Taking a scented sprig and letting people have a whiff of the wonderful piney aroma. There was no time for food, no time to rest. It was frustrating trying to get strangers to listen, but worse yet would be to return home empty-handed. When someone offered us fifty dollars, when another offered forty, we took what we could get. We had no time to haggle. Fifteen dollars? We took it, none too happy. How about ten? I'm afraid so. Tree after tree was lifted off the truck, until the last one was sold for five dollars. Some people lashed their new tree to the roof of their cars, others dragged them down the street, leaving a sweeping path in the snow.

Our faces and fingers and toes frozen, we took some of the money and bought ourselves some clam chowder to go. "So how'd we do?" Kate asked as she drove the truck toward I-93 north.

I counted the money, then counted it again. "Four hundred and sixty-five dollars," I told her.

"Not bad for a couple of amateurs," she said with a grin. "You keep ten and I'll keep ten, and we'll give the rest to Mom and Dad." So our trip to Boston wasn't a total flop. What sadness I felt at losing the spruces was made up by knowing we'd have enough money to get us through the holidays.

By the time we had driven clear of the city, it was nearing ten o'clock. The traffic was quiet. For the most part, people were in bed, long asleep.

"Are you all right to drive?" I asked Kate.

"I'm fine," she said and I believed her. "Quite a one-day adventure," she added. "And to think we thought we'd come home with two thousand dollars!"

This wasn't that funny—but we both laughed.

"Well, the money will help," I said.

"Call me crazy, Willie," she said, "but I think the worst to happen has already happened to me."

"Buy something for Shelly," I said, handing her a twenty-dollar bill.

"Are you sure?" Kate asked.

"Yes, I'm sure. Something warm for the winter. So maybe she—and you and me—can sleep at night." I bunched up a blanket and used it as a pillow against the side door.

"Willie, I'm glad we had this day," she said. Again I waited for some smart comment to follow. But there wasn't any. Instead, we rehashed the day, remembering things to tell Mom and Dad.

I don't know exactly what time we arrived home. I don't remember because I soon fell asleep in the truck and slept most of the way.

I don't recall my sister Kate carrying me inside. But she said she did and that's good enough for me.

I do remember waking up in my own warm bed. Waking up to the smell of our own maple syrup and to pancakes cooking.

That next morning, with the trip to Boston and back already a dreamlike whirl, I looked out my window, expecting for just a moment to see the spruces across the road. Instead I saw the stumps like small grave markers in the snow.

This sad image might have stayed with me if I hadn't walked into the living room and seen our own Christmas tree, tall and decorated. For then I realized that people in Boston were waking to admire the beautiful spruces they had bought from Kate and me. Trees that their neighbors and friends would envy. Trees that children would dress with strings of paper chains or popcorn, with tinsel and their own special ornaments.

Trees that would bring to the dense heart of winter the reminder of life, full and fragrant.

Extending Comprehension

Story Questions

1. Why does the Johnston family look forward to the profits from the fall sugaring season?
2. Why is the fall sugaring season the worst in memory?
3. What kinds of staples does the family stock up on?
4. Why does Dad tell Kate to get off the interstate highway?
5. Why does Kate hate being home again?
6. What does Willie suggest as a way for the family to earn some money?
7. What is Dad's objection?
8. During the long drive to Boston, Kate talks about the mess she has made of her life. What are some of her concerns?
9. What else do she and her brother talk about?
10. When they finally arrive in Boston, Kate and her brother discover it isn't easy to find a parking place. They finally park in Harvard Square. One man tells them this isn't a good place to sell trees. Why?
11. When they find a new place, another man tells them, "We control this part of the territory." What does he mean?
12. Finally, they find themselves in a ritzy part of Boston. What kind people do you find in a ritzy part of a city?
13. Why don't they get a check from the lady in a fur coat?
14. The police officer says they need a commercial license and an interstate permit to sell trees. Why do you think they didn't have these papers?
15. The police officer decides to give them an hour to sell the trees. What do Kate and her brother do?
16. What do you think Kate means when she says, "Call me crazy, Willie, but I think the worst to happen has already happened to me."

Discussion Topics

1. Dad says, "The cost of being alive is simply so high." How does the author let you know that the Johnston family is having trouble getting enough money to pay the cost of being alive?

   During your discussion, tell how the different family members talk about not having enough money. Start with Dad's remark "The cost of being alive is simply so high."

2. Even though the people in the narrator's family sometimes have problems getting along, they also help each other. What are some ways that one family member helps another family member?

   As you discuss how they help each other, give some examples from the story. Talk about:

   - how Willie helps his father
   - how Willie helps Kate
   - how Kate helps her father
   - how Willie and Kate help their parents

3. Willie and his father cut down twenty-five beautiful spruce trees so that they can sell them. Discuss the following questions:

   - Do you think they should have kept the trees and found other ways to earn money?
   - Do you think they did the right thing by cutting and selling the trees?

Writing Ideas

1. The author writes many sentences about how cold it is in Vermont in December. Here are two sentences:

   "The limbs of bare birch trees were coated with crusty week-old snow. The river, a frozen gray, like trapped smoke, looked so cold that I wondered how fish could survive."

   - Copy these sentences and then look through the story to find more sentences that let you know how cold it is. Write down at least five of those sentences or groups of sentences. Then make up sentences of your own. Read your sentences out loud to your classmates. See if they shiver while they are listening to the sentences you wrote.

2. In the last part of the story, Willie thinks about the people in Boston who bought their trees. He thinks, "Trees that would bring to the dense heart of winter the reminder of life, full and fragrant." What do you think he means? Write your interpretation of what Willie is talking about.

Additional Reading

The Black Stallion

Section 1 (Chapters 1–5)
Word List

tramp steamer	eerie
prow	monotonously
missionary	turban
gangplank	makeshift
tersely	clambered
accommodation	stud
inert	careening
bureau	broadside
subside	grazed
swerved	circumference
parched	hypnotize
prone	adjoining
edible	strove
sustain	venomous
gelatinous	ravine
rhythmic	horsemanship
incredulous	bedlam
blunt	

Questions

1. At the beginning of the novel, was the stallion wild or tame?
2. Where would the stallion rather be, in a cage or in a field?
3. The stallion came from ____.
   - America
   - India
   - Arabia
4. What happened to the *Drake* during the storm?
5. Who pulled Alec to the island?
6. Alec finally landed on the island. What would have happened to him if he had not been able to cut the rope?
7. Alec struggled to survive on the island.
   a. What food did he find on bushes?
   b. What did he make from driftwood?
   c. Why did he make a spear?
   d. What was the name of the seaweed that Alec ate?
8. On the island, how did the stallion save Alec's life?
9. What happened to Alec the first two times he tried to ride the stallion?
10. How did the stallion change after Alec was able to ride him?
11. What attracted the ship's attention to the island?
12. Why didn't the captain want to take the stallion on the ship?
13. Why did Alec have to fasten a band around the stallion's waist?
14. What happened to Alec's leg?

Section 2 (Chapters 6–9)
Word List

uncanny	taut
mingle	instinctive
antiseptic	supremacy
queasy	iron constitution
clean bill of health	spry
clamored their	self-reliant
wares	earmark
yarn	blessing in disguise
beseechingly	rumpus
resignedly	astride

Questions

1. On which continent is Rio de Janeiro?
2. On which continent is New York City?
3. What did Alec buy with the money his parents sent him?
4. When Alec was boarding the ship for New York, why did the stallion break away from him?
5. Why did Alec need to use antiseptic on the stallion?
6. On the ship to New York, why didn't Alec stay in his cabin?
7. What did the stallion do to one of the quarantine inspectors?
8. Why did Alec have to blindfold the stallion on the New York dock?

9. What was Joe Russo's job?
10. Why was Joe Russo so interested in Alec and the stallion?
11. What kind of building did the stallion live in?
12. Who owned that building?
13. Which other horse lived in that building?
14. What kind of effect did the other horse have on the stallion?
15. What scared the stallion in the middle of the night?
16. Henry thought the stallion would be good at a particular sport. Which sport?
17. What kind of experience did Henry have with that sport?
18. What did the stallion do at the end of this section?

Section 3 (Chapters 10–14)
Word List

fairway	gully
staccato	burrs
aroma	sire
dam	registered
pedigree	sheepishly
tutelage	withers
shied	vapor
cinch	contrary
slacken	skittishly
idolized	veteran
jowls	conscientiously
extensive	prophesying
retaliate	charity

Questions

1. Why did Alec think that the stallion would come to the pool?
2. Why didn't Alec tell his mother about the stallion running away?
3. Why did Alec need to get registration papers for the stallion?
4. Why would it be difficult to get those papers?

5. On the first of April, Henry and Alec started training the stallion to do what?
6. Which object did they put on the stallion's back?
7. Why didn't the stallion like that object?
8. What kind of place did Henry and Alec take the stallion to at one o'clock in the morning?
9. Why did they bring Napoleon along?
10. Why do you think the stallion loved the track so much?
11. What bad news did the letter bring?
12. Which two horses were going to race in Chicago?
13. Why did Joe Russo think that the stallion could enter that race?
14. Why did Joe Russo want to bring Jim Neville to the track?

Section 4 (Chapters 15–18)
Word List

shindig	brusquely
circulating	foremost
gain momentum	authorities
pulses	delirious
stupendous	faltering
cocky	temperamental
paddock	streamlined
vantage point	plaintively
superficial wound	mount

Questions

1. Was Jim Neville impressed with the stallion?
2. In his column, Jim Neville said that the race in Chicago would no longer prove who was the fastest horse. Why was that?
3. What did the other owners finally agree to do?
4. When Alec told his father about the race, he signaled Henry to come over. Why do you think Alec wanted Henry to talk to his father?

5. What did Alec have to finish before leaving for Chicago?
6. The stallion refused to leave New York unless another animal came with him. Which animal was that?
7. How did Alec and the others get to Chicago?
8. Before the race, how did the other jockeys treat Alec?
9. How did the crowd react when they saw the stallion?
10. What did the stallion do with Sun Raider before the race?
11. What did Sun Raider do to the stallion's leg?
12. Why didn't the stallion start the race with the other horses?
13. In which part of the race did the stallion pass the other horses?
14. Was the stallion's wound serious?
15. Who was the fastest horse in the world?

Writing Assignment

Write a story that explains where the black stallion came from. Make your story at least ten sentences long.

Centerburg Tales

Grandpa Hercules
Word List

nib	disdainfully
commence	monument
contraption	axle
tread water	pelts
feenomina	putting on airs
(phenomenon)	peetition (petition)
get your	endorsement
dander up	elaborated
yarn	statistic
enriched	knoll

Questions

1. Grampa Herc told a story about a raft trip he took. What did he say stopped his raft in the middle of the creek?

2. Could that really have happened?
3. Explain your answer to question 2.
4. Why did Uncle Ulysses have seventy-two boxes of Whoopsy-Doodles without box tops?
5. Grampa Herc told a story about how he supported a bridge. What did he say happened to the ice he was standing on?
6. So how did he keep standing up?
7. Could that really have happened?
8. Explain your answer to question 7.
9. Grampa Herc told a story about a clock. What did he say was making the clock run slowly?
10. Grampa Herc told a story about panning for gold. In which state was he panning for gold?
11. What made Hopper McThud heavier each time he jumped across the stream?
12. So what happened to Hopper McThud when he took off his clothes?
13. Could that really have happened?
14. Explain your answer to question 13.
15. Mr. Gabby sent Grampa Herc a carton of Gravity-Bitties breakfast food. What was the bottom of each Gravity-Bitty box made out of?
16. According to the directions, you first had to _____ the Gravity-Bitties. Then you had to pin the _____ inside your coat. Then you had to practice _____.
17. Grampa Herc finally jumped in the middle of March. To which state did he jump?
18. At first, did Uncle Ulysses believe that Grampa Herc had jumped that far?
19. Why did Uncle Ulysses change his mind after he saw the package?
20. Who do you think sent the package?

Experiment 13
Word List

strop
fertilizer
pollen
complacent
savings bonds
pruned
subversive

Questions

1. What was Dulcy Dooner's uncle famous for?
2. What did Dulcy Dooner inherit from his uncle?
3. Why did everybody think those objects might be valuable?
4. In what kind of house did Dulcy plant his seeds?
5. Why did Homer and Freddy have to knock holes in the roof of that house?
6. At first, how did Dulcy try to make money from the plants?
7. Why did Dulcy's first plan for making money fail?
8. What kinds of plants did Dulcy's plants turn out to be?
9. What fever does that plant give to people?
10. Why did everybody want to leave town?
11. At the meeting, Dulcy made a deal with the town. What would the town pay Dulcy to do?
12. Why didn't Dulcy keep the money he made from this deal?
13. Homer figured out what would happen if an enemy planted the seeds.
    a. What would everybody in the country be doing after that?
    b. So what would happen to all the activity in the country?
14. The sheriff was going to throw away the seeds in a particular place. Which place?
15. How did Homer get rid of the seeds instead?

16. The number **13** is very important in this story. Name at least three things that involved the number **13**.

Ever So Much More So
Word List

awning
elixir
pompous
unadulterated
sanitary
metamorphosis
led astray
exceedingly
attributable
instantaneous
texture
impurities
cerebral
absorbent

Questions

1. What product was Professor Ear selling?
2. According to Professor Ear, when you sprinkled that product on a doughnut, the doughnut tasted _____ delicious.
3. How long was one can of that product supposed to last?
4. The next week, each character was ever so much more like himself.
   a. Which character was ever so much more pompous?
   b. Which character was ever so much more lazy?
   c. Which character was ever so much more uncooperative?
   d. Which character was ever so much more flustered and suspicious?
5. All of those characters felt that Professor Ear had _____ them.
6. Grampa Hercules knew what was really in each can.
   a. How did he feel about that product?
   b. What did he convince the other characters to do?
7. The professor's full name gives you a clue about what EVERSOMUCH MORE-SO really was. The professor's full name was Atmos P. H. Ear.
   a. What word does that name sound like?

b. So what was in each can?

c. So Grampa Hercules loved EVERSOMUCH MORE-SO because he loved the_____.

8. According to this story, what are the important things in life?

Pie and Punch and You-Know-Whats
Word List

hypnotize	amethyst
reproachfully	martyr
tinge	cadenza
forte	periodicals
quartet	brandishing
vestibule	septets
predicament	precariously
monotonous	Dewey Decimal
spasmodic	System

Questions

1. At the beginning of the story, what machine kept changing colors?
2. What object did the stranger bring into the lunchroom?
3. The stranger called the boys a "parturient pair of panted Pandoras."
   a. What does "parturient" mean?
   b. Pandora was a woman who let trouble out of a box. So what would a "panted Pandora" be?
   c. In this story, which box does the trouble come out of?
4. What did the boys start doing after they heard the sound?
5. Could the boys control what they were doing?
6. What happened to all the people who heard the boys?
7. Homer knew there was a cure in a story by _____.
8. Which building did all the people go to?
9. Homer finally found the new poem. What happened to him when he told everybody the new poem?
10. Why did everybody tell the new poem to the sixth-grade teacher?

11. What would the sixth-grade teacher have to do to cure herself?
12. The sheriff played the song on the flip side of the record.
    a. Which animals did that song tell about?
    b. That song gave you the _____.

Writing Assignment

Which story did you like best? Write a paragraph that explains your answer. Make your paragraph at least ten sentences long.

Charlotte's Web
Section 1 (Chapters 1–6)
Word List

a fine specimen	scythes
glutton	stealthily
objectionable	unremitting
lair	

Questions

1. At the beginning of the novel, why was Mr. Arable going to kill Wilbur?
2. How did Fern give Wilbur milk?
3. What kind of person gets milk that way?
4. What is a spring pig?
5. Which family bought Wilbur when he was five weeks old?
6. Which building did Wilbur live in on their place?
7. Name at least three other animals that lived in the building.
8. What would Fern do when she came to that building?
9. One afternoon, what did a goose convince Wilbur to do?
10. Why did the animals' suggestions confuse Wilbur when he was outside?
11. How did Mr. Zuckerman get Wilbur back into the barn?
12. Wilbur made careful plans for the next day. What ruined his plans?

13. Wilbur told the lamb that there couldn't be anything that was less than nothing. Explain how Wilbur reached that conclusion.
14. Wilbur was unhappy because he needed something. What was that?
15. Who offered to be Wilbur's friend?
16. What did Charlotte like to drink?
17. Why was it difficult for Wilbur to like Charlotte at first?
18. What important event happened to the goose?
19. Which object did Templeton roll away?
20. What would that object be like if it broke?

Section 2 (Chapters 7–11)
Word List
detested	loathed
anesthetic	conspiracy
buckboards	

Questions

1. The old sheep explained Mr. Zuckerman's plans to Wilbur. What did Mr. Zuckerman plan to do with Wilbur?
2. What did Charlotte say she would do for Wilbur?
3. Why was Mrs. Arable worried about Fern?
4. Mr. Arable said, "Maybe our ears aren't as sharp as Fern's." What did he mean by that?
5. Wilbur boasted that he could make something that Charlotte made. What was that?
6. How did Wilbur try to make that thing?
7. Were Wilbur's efforts successful?
8. How did Wilbur feel about life and the world?
9. What did Avery try to do to Charlotte?
10. Why was there such a rotten smell in the air after Avery did that?

11. How did the smell save Charlotte's life?
12. The next morning, which two words did Charlotte write in her web?
13. Why did the people think that was a miracle?
14. Why did everybody come to the Zuckermans' farm?
15. Why did Fern think that the barn was less pleasant now?

Section 3 (Chapters 12–17)
Word List
baser instincts	destiny
adjourn	rummaging
incessant	reputation
forsake	veritable treasure
yarn	surpass
stowaway	pummel
lacerated	listless

Questions

1. At the meeting, Charlotte explained why she had written the words in her web. Why had she written them?
2. Why wouldn't Mr. Zuckerman want to kill Wilbur now?
3. Why did Charlotte want to write a new word?
4. What did Charlotte want Templeton to get for her?
5. How did Templeton depend upon Wilbur?
6. What was the next word that Charlotte wrote?
7. Which event did Mr. Zuckerman decide to take Wilbur to?
8. Where did the words "with new radiant action" come from?
9. Charlotte told Wilbur a story about a cousin of hers and a fish. What happened in the story?
10. Why did Mrs. Arable go to visit Dr. Dorian?
11. What did Dr. Dorian think the real miracle was?

12. Dr. Dorian thought there was a reason he never heard animals talking. What was the reason?
13. What was the next word that Charlotte wrote in her web?
14. What did the crickets sing about?
15. Why did Charlotte need to build a sac?
16. What kind of bath did Mrs. Zuckerman give Wilbur?
17. How did the sheep convince Templeton to go to the fair?
18. What did Mr. Arable say that made Wilbur faint?
19. At the fair, what was the pig next to Wilbur like?
20. Why did Charlotte think that pig would be hard for Wilbur to beat?
21. How did Charlotte plan to help Wilbur?

Section 4 (Chapters 18–22)
Word List

schemer	carousing
gorge	confetti
sentiments	hallowed

Questions

1. Why was Mrs. Arable so happy when she saw Fern on the Ferris wheel?
2. What was the last word that Charlotte made in her web?
3. What other object did Charlotte make?
4. Why wouldn't Charlotte ever see her children?
5. Which pig won first prize?
6. What kind of prize did Wilbur win?
7. After Wilbur won the prize, who was Fern more interested in?
8. What made Wilbur faint again?
9. What was the greatest moment in Mr. Zuckerman's life?
10. What did Charlotte tell Wilbur that made him cry?
11. What did Wilbur want Templeton to get for him?

12. What deal did Wilbur make with Templeton?
13. How did Wilbur carry the egg sac back home?
14. What happened to Charlotte after Wilbur left?
15. Why did Wilbur know that Mr. Zuckerman would keep him for as long as he lived?
16. What happened to Templeton because of his deal with Wilbur?
17. What came out of Charlotte's sac one day?
18. How did most of the spiders leave the barn?
19. How many spiders stayed in the barn?
20. How did Fern change?
21. How did Wilbur feel about the barn?
22. Charlotte was in a class by herself because she had two important qualities. Name those two qualities.

Writing Assignment

The people in the book thought that Charlotte's writing was a miracle. Do you believe in miracles? Write a paragraph that explains your answer. Make your paragraph at least ten sentences long.

Mrs. Frisby and the Rats of NIMH

Section 1 (Chapters 1–7)
Word List

cinder block	prospect
texture	cocoon
filtering	eaves
fare	idling
warily	plummet
parsnip	primeval
corn shuck	sonorous
authoritatively	access
pallet	rancid
roundabout	depressed
botanically	sward

furrowed
protrude
lath
hypochondriac
relentlessly
hermit
delirious

capacity
harrow
reputation
essence
expedition
slither
dietary

Questions

1. What kind of object did Mrs. Frisby and her family live in?
2. What kind of garden was that object in?
3. Why didn't Timothy join his family for breakfast?
4. Why did Mrs. Frisby go to see Mr. Ages?
5. Why did Mrs. Frisby take such a roundabout way to Mr. Ages' house?
6. What kinds of things did Mr. Ages collect in his sack?
7. What disease did Timothy have?
8. What problem did the crow have?
9. How did Mrs. Frisby free the crow?
10. How did the crow help Mrs. Frisby in return?
11. Why would the Frisby family have to move out of the garden?
12. What might happen to Timothy if the Frisby family moved?
13. Mrs. Frisby found out about Mr. Fitzgibbon's plans. How many days did she have left to move her family?
14. When Mrs. Frisby was coming home, the cat did something unusual. What was that?
15. Mrs. Frisby saw some rats. What were they doing?
16. Where did the crow take Mrs. Frisby at dusk one evening?
17. Describe what the owl's home was like.

Section 2 (Chapters 8–14)
Word List

deference
lamely
domain
intertwined
hostile
laboriously
pry
recounted
contritely

conceivably
prowl
trespassers
rarity
urgent
explicit
incomprehensible
baffled
entranced

Questions

1. The owl became very interested in Mrs. Frisby after she told him something. What did she tell him?
2. What did the owl think that the rats could do with Mrs. Frisby's house?
3. What is the lee side of a barn?
4. What sort of bush did the rats live under?
5. What was Brutus guarding?
6. Why did Mrs. Frisby begin to leave the rosebush?
7. Why was Mrs. Frisby able to see when they were far under ground?
8. What did Mrs. Frisby and the others take instead of the stairs?
9. In what kind of room did Mrs. Frisby wait for the others?
10. What did Mrs. Frisby think was so unusual about the rats?
11. Why did Mrs. Frisby know how to read?
12. Nicodemus figured out what the lee side of the stone was. What was it?
13. How did the rats usually protect themselves from the cat?
14. What task did Mrs. Frisby volunteer to do?
15. What had happened to Mr. Frisby when he had done that?
16. Describe what Nicodemus's room was like.
17. Where had Nicodemus grown up?
18. Where did he get his food?
19. What did the people from the NIMH truck do to Nicodemus one night?

Section 3 (Chapters 15–21)
Word List

inextricably	portal
futile	case the place
scientifically	undergo
compiled	injection
biologist	maze
illusion	at large
wryly	underestimating
dictated	inkling
unerringly	undoing
ritual	astute
foresee	shafts
plaintive	consternation
pry	roving
open	satchel
cursory	debated
primarily	

Questions

1. What kind of place were Nicodemus and the other rats taken to?
2. What were Dr. Schultz and the others doing with the rats?
3. How did Dr. Schultz put liquid into the rats?
4. What was the first kind of test that Nicodemus took?
5. What did that test tell Dr. Schultz about the rats?
6. What did Justin try to do one day?
7. How was the A group different from the other two groups?
8. What had made them different?
9. Which other group of animals was like the A group of rats?
10. What did Dr. Schultz teach the rats to do with words?
11. Why did Justin know how to open his cage?
12. What passageway did Justin discover behind the baseboard?
13. Where did that passageway lead?
14. Why did the rats use string when they explored the passageway?
15. What happened to six of the mice in the passageway?
16. How did the other two mice help the rats escape?
17. How did the rats learn while they were at the Boniface Estate?
18. What kinds of things did Mrs. Frisby see in the main hall?
19. What were the rats going to use the plow for?
20. For the Plan, the rats would live without _____.
21. After they left the Boniface Estate, the rats decided to live _____ the ground.
22. Which dead person did the rats find?

Section 4 (Chapters 22–28)
Word List

precautions	exterminate
cynical	pessimist
irrigation	drought
denounce	admonish
colander	electrocuted
insulation	short circuit
federal government	epidemic
cyanide	deposit
exert	impasse
commence	hillock
pulleys	precision
cryptically	dispatch
flexed	cleated
stubble	incredulously

Questions

1. What useful things did the rats find in the Toy Tinker's truck?
2. How did the rats get electricity for their cave?
3. Why did the rats become discontented with their life?
4. Why did the rats fear Mr. Fitzgibbon?
5. One day, Nicodemus took Jenner to a place in the woods. What was the name of that place?
6. Why was Nicodemus interested in that place?
7. Why didn't Jenner agree with Nicodemus's plan?

8. Why did Jenner leave the other rats?
9. Why did Mrs. Frisby go to the cat's bowl?
10. What did Bill Fitzgibbon do to Mrs. Frisby after she did that?
11. Mrs. Frisby found out what had happened to the other rats.
    a. What were they trying to take from the hardware store?
    b. What killed them?
    c. Why was the government so interested in those rats?
    d. What was the government going to do for Mr. Fitzgibbon?
12. Who rescued Mrs. Frisby from the birdcage?
13. What did the rats do for Mrs. Frisby after she escaped from the birdcage?
14. Why did the rats destroy their home before they left it?
15. Why did ten of the rats stay behind?
16. Before some of those rats escaped into the woods, they ran around in circles. Why did they do that?
17. Where did Mrs. Frisby and her family move to later that year?
18. Where were they thinking about moving at the end of the novel?

Writing Assignment

Do you think that animals could be as smart as people? Write a paragraph that explains your answer. Make your paragraph at least ten sentences long.

Caddie Woodlawn

Section 1 (Chapters 1–6)
Word List

inseparable	sedate
massacre	cameo brooch
virtues	escapade
relenting	victuals
calico	christening
sheaths	irksome
unpardonable	unfathomable

abolition	fervor
reproachfully	sampler
wholesale	incite
slaughter	enthrall
moderation	benediction
sheepishly	pendulum
ruefully	genial
reverberated	aristocrats
deft bribe	vibrant
salvage	glutton
pompously	Cheshire cat
loons	ominously
fowl	fife and drum corps
seamstress	treading
denim	inefficient
muffler	infamy
pommeling	silhouetted
pioneer	wheedle
scalp belt	enterprise
irresolutely	barbarous
pitch	billows
pliable	challis
venison	clannish
disheveled	admonish

Questions

1. Did Caddie act like the other girls in her family?
2. Which family members did Caddie play with and act like?
3. Who wanted Caddie to run wild, her mother or father?
4. Which Native American was friendly with Caddie?
5. What did the Circuit Rider do for a living?
6. What did Caddie do to disgrace herself when she met the Circuit Rider?
7. What did the Circuit Rider ask Mr. Woodlawn to repair?
8. Which birds did the people hunt?
9. The writer compared those birds to a group of people who were fighting a losing battle with the white people. Which people were like the birds?

10. What was Uncle Edmund always doing to people?
11. What did Uncle Edmund do to Caddie's raft?
12. Why did Uncle Edmund give Caddie a silver dollar?
13. Why did Uncle Edmund take Nero with him?
14. During which season did school begin?
15. Why didn't school go on all year round?
16. What did the teacher do to Obediah Jones in front of the class?
17. How did Obediah treat the teacher after that incident?

Section 2 (Chapters 7–12)
Word List

tumultuous	pored over
rivalry	exasperation
compartments	draughty
accumulate	breeches
clogs	hassocks
murals	pursed his lips
thrifty	miserly
beau	indolent
elation	inconsolable
in her element	boastful
smelling salts	

Questions

1. What happened to Caddie when she went skating on thin ice?
2. Why did Caddie have to stay inside for most of the winter?
3. What skill did Caddie learn from her father that winter?
4. Was Mr. Woodlawn's English family royal or ordinary?
5. Why was Mr. Woodlawn's father ordered to leave that family?
6. What did Mr. Woodlawn do to earn money for his mother and father?
7. Why do you think that Mr. Woodlawn did not want to go back to England?

8. What deal did the Woodlawn children make with the Hankinson children?
9. Why were the Woodlawn children happy with that deal?
10. What bad news was in Uncle Edmund's letter?
11. What rumor did Mr. Kent bring to the Woodlawns?
12. Why did all the neighbors gather at the Woodlawns' house?
13. Caddie overheard some men talking about the Indians. What did those men want to do to the Native Americans?
14. Why did Caddie go to see Indian John?
15. What did the Native Americans plan to do the next day?
16. Who met Caddie on her way back home?
17. What did Mr. Woodlawn and John agree to do?

Section 3 (Chapters 13–18)
Word List

portage	incredulously
confirmation	partridge
meter	arbutus
inadvertently	bunting
conspicuously	foreboding
furrows	novelty
good riddance	

Questions

1. Why were the Native Americans moving westward for a time?
2. Which two presents did Indian John give Caddie?
3. How did the children plan to make money from the scalp belt?
4. Why did Mrs. Hankinson have to leave town?
5. What did Caddie do with her silver dollar?
6. Even though she didn't buy anything for herself, Caddie felt she'd gotten her dollar's worth. Why?

7. What did Robert Ireton do to entertain the children?
8. Why had Katie Hyman become sick?
9. Why was Tom so embarrassed when his eyes met Katie's?
10. What did the students have to perform on "speaking" day?
11. What was wrong with Warren's performance?
12. During the storm, what happened to the oak tree right after the children left it?
13. Tom told the story of Pee Wee.
    a. What did Pee Wee end up getting for his dead oxen?
    b. What did Pee Wee end up getting for his dead wife?
    c. Why did Pee Wee get all the farmers' land?
14. Why was Hetty so happy to be with Caddie?
15. What terrible news did the Circuit Rider bring?

Section 4 (Chapters 19–24)
Word List

churning	apparition
city airs	pandemonium
conviction	stupendous
culprits	remorse
plaintive	tremulously

Questions

1. What kind of language did Annabelle use in her letter?
2. What did Indian John's dog warn the school about?
3. How did Obediah and the other boys keep the fire away from the school?
4. Annabelle wanted to be as un_____ as the Woodlawn children.
5. What did the sheep do to Annabelle as she held the salt?
6. What trick did Caddie play on Annabelle in the hayloft?
7. Why was Caddie singled out for punishment?

8. What was Caddie planning to do before her father came to see her?
9. Caddie's father thought that women should teach men certain ways to behave. Name some of those ways.
10. What news did the letter from England bring?
11. What kinds of things would the family gain if they moved to England?
12. What kinds of things would the family have to give up if they moved to England?
13. How did the family decide what to do?
14. Why do you think they decided to stay?
15. Which traveler came home at the end of the novel?
16. The last sentence of the novel says that Caddie Woodlawn was a _____ and an _____.

Writing Assignment
Caddie Woodlawn and Tom Sawyer are alike in many ways, and different in other ways. Write a paragraph that compares Caddie Woodlawn and Tom Sawyer. Make your paragraph at least ten sentences long.